AF619589

No Other Gods Before Me:
Contrasting False Worship with the True God

John Calvin; Caleb Sinclair

Published by

GRAPEVINE INDIA PUBLISHERS PVT LTD

www.grapevineindia.com
Delhi | Mumbai
email: grapevineindiapublishers@gmail.com

Ordering Information:
Quantity sales: Special discounts are available on quantity purchases by corporations, associations, and others.
For details, reach out to the publisher.

First published by Grapevine India 2023
Copyright © Grapevine 2023
All rights reserved

Welcome to our Christian book collection!

For access to more Christian audiobooks,

send a blank email to

thegoodchristian10@gmail.com.

Contents

1.

The Nature and Tendency of the Knowledge of God.

By the knowledge of God, I intend not merely a notion that there is such a Being, but also an acquaintance with whatever we ought to know concerning Him, conducing to his glory and our benefit. For we cannot with propriety say, there is any knowledge of God where there is no religion or piety. I have no reference here to that species of knowledge by which men, lost and condemned in themselves, apprehend God the Redeemer in Christ the Mediator; but only to that first and simple knowledge, to which the genuine order of nature would lead us, if Adam had retained his innocence. For though, in the present ruined state of human nature, no man will ever perceive God to be a Father, or the Author of salvation, or in any respect propitious, but as pacified by the mediation of Christ; yet it is one thing to understand, that God our Maker supports us by his power, governs us by his providence, nourishes us by his goodness, and follows us with blessings of every kind, and another to embrace the grace of reconciliation proposed to us in Christ. Therefore, since God is first manifested, both in the structure of the world and in the general tenor of Scripture, simply as the Creator, and afterwards reveals himself in the person of Christ as a Redeemer, hence arises a twofold knowledge of him; of which the former is first to be considered, and the other will follow in its proper place. For though our mind cannot conceive of God, without ascribing some worship to him, it will not be sufficient merely to apprehend that he is the only proper object of universal worship and adoration, unless we are also persuaded that he is the fountain of all good, and seek for none but in him. This I maintain, not only because he sustains the universe, as he once made it, by his infinite power, governs it by his wisdom, preserves it by his goodness, and especially reigns over the human race in righteousness and judgment, exercising a merciful forbearance, and defending them by his protection; but because there cannot be found the least particle of wisdom, light, righteousness, power, rectitude, or sincere truth which does not proceed from him, and claim him for its author: we should therefore learn to expect and supplicate all these things from him, and thankfully to acknowledge what he gives us. For this sense of the divine perfections is calculated to teach us piety, which produces religion. By piety, I mean a reverence and love of God, arising from a knowledge of his benefits. For, till men are sensible that they owe every thing to God, that they are supported by his paternal care, that he is the Author of all the blessings they enjoy, and that nothing should be sought independently of him, they will never voluntarily submit to his authority; they will never truly and cordially devote themselves to his service, unless they rely upon him alone for true felicity.

II. Cold and frivolous, then, are the speculations of those who employ themselves in disquisitions on the essence of God, when it would be more interesting to us to become acquainted with his character, and to know what is agreeable to his nature. For what end is answered by professing, with Epicurus, that there is a God, who, discarding all concern about the world, indulges himself in perpetual inactivity? What benefit arises from the knowledge of a God with whom we have no concern? Our knowledge of God should rather tend, first, to teach us fear and reverence; and, secondly, to instruct us to implore all good at his hand, and to render him the praise of all that we receive. For how can you entertain a thought of God without immediately reflecting, that, being a creature of his formation, you must, by right of creation, be subject to his authority? that you are indebted to him for your life, and that all your actions should be done with reference to him? If this be true, it certainly follows that your life is miserably corrupt, unless it be regulated by a desire of obeying him, since his will ought to be the rule of our conduct. Nor can you have a clear view of him without discovering him to be the fountain and origin of all good. This would produce a desire of union to him, and confidence in him, if the human mind were not seduced by its own depravity from the right path of investigation. For, even at the first, the pious mind dreams not of any imaginary deity, but contemplates only the one true God; and, concerning him, indulges not the fictions of fancy, but, content with believing him to be such as he reveals himself, uses the most diligent and unremitting caution, lest it should fall into error by a rash and presumptuous transgression of his will. He who thus knows him, sensible that all things are subject to his control, confides in him as his Guardian and Protector, and unreservedly commits himself to his care. Assured that he is the author of all blessings, in distress or want he immediately flies to his protection, and expects his aid. Persuaded of his goodness and mercy, he relies on him with unlimited confidence, nor doubts of finding in his clemency a remedy provided for all his evils. Knowing him to be his Lord and Father, he concludes that he ought to mark his government in all things, revere his majesty, endeavour to promote his glory, and obey his commands. Perceiving him to be a just Judge, armed with severity for the punishment of crimes, he keeps his tribunal always in view, and is restrained by fear from provoking his wrath. Yet he is not so terrified at the apprehension of his justice, as to wish to evade it, even if escape were possible; but loves him as much in punishing the wicked as in blessing the pious, because he believes it as necessary to his glory to punish the impious and abandoned, as to reward the righteous with eternal life. Besides, he restrains himself from sin, not merely from a dread of vengeance, but because he loves and reveres God as his Father, honours and worships him as his Lord, and, even though there were no hell, would shudder at the thought of offending him. See, then, the nature of pure and genuine religion. It consists in faith, united with a serious fear of God, comprehending a voluntary reverence, and producing legitimate worship agreeable to the injunctions of the law. And this requires to be the more carefully remarked, because men in general render to God a formal worship, but very few truly reverence him; while great ostentation in ceremonies is universally displayed, but sincerity of heart is rarely to be found.

2.

All Idolatrous Worship Discountenanced in The Scripture, by Its Exclusive Opposition of the True God to All the Fictitious Deities of the Heathen.

But, since we have shown that the knowledge of God, which is otherwise exhibited without obscurity in the structure of the world, and in all the creatures, is yet more familiarly and clearly unfolded in the word, it will be useful to examine, whether the representation, which the Lord gives us of himself in the Scripture, agrees with the portraiture which he had before been pleased to delineate in his works. This is indeed an extensive subject, if we intended to dwell on a particular discussion of it. But I shall content myself with suggesting some hints, by which the minds of the pious may learn what ought to be their principal objects of investigation in Scripture concerning God, and may be directed to a certain end in that inquiry. I do not yet allude to the peculiar covenant which distinguished the descendants of Abraham from the rest of the nations. For in receiving, by gratuitous adoption, those who were his enemies into the number of his children, God even then manifested himself as a Redeemer; but we are still treating of that knowledge which relates to the creation of the world, without ascending to Christ the Mediator. But though it will be useful soon to cite some passages from the New Testament, (since that also demonstrates the power of God in the creation, and his providence in the conservation of the world,) yet I wish the reader to be apprized of the point now intended to be discussed, that he may not pass the limits which the subject prescribes. At present, then, let it suffice to understand how God, the former of heaven and earth, governs the world which he hath made. Both his paternal goodness, and the beneficent inclinations of his will, are everywhere celebrated; and examples are given of his severity, which discover him to be the righteous punisher of iniquities, especially where his forbearance produces no salutary effects upon the obstinate.

II. In some places, indeed, we are favoured with more explicit descriptions, which exhibit to our view an exact representation of his genuine countenance. For Moses, in the description which he gives of it, certainly appears to have intended a brief comprehension of all that it was possible for men to know concerning him—"The Lord, the Lord God, merciful and gracious, long suffering, and abundant in goodness and truth, keeping mercy for thousands, forgiving iniquity, and transgression, and sin, and that will by no means clear the guilty; visiting the iniquity of the fathers upon the children, and upon the children's children." Where we may observe, first, the assertion of his eternity and self-existence, in that magnificent name, which is twice repeated; and secondly, the celebration of his attributes, giving us a description, not of what he is in himself, but of what he is to us, that our knowledge of him may consist rather in a lively perception, than in vain and airy speculation. Here we find an enumeration of the same perfections which, as we have remarked, are illustriously displayed both in heaven and on earth—clemency, goodness, mercy, justice, judgment, and truth. For power is comprised in the word Elohim, God. The prophets distinguish him by the same epithets, when they intend a complete exhibition of his holy name. But, to avoid the necessity of quoting many passages, let us content ourselves at present with referring to one Psalm; which contains such an accurate summary of all his perfections, that nothing seems to be omitted. And yet it contains nothing but what may be known from a contemplation of the creatures. Thus, by the teaching of experience, we perceive God to be just what he declares himself in his word. In Jeremiah, where he announces in what characters he will be known by us, he gives a description, not so full, but to the same effect—"Let him that glorieth glory in this, that he understandeth and knoweth me, that I am the Lord, which exercise loving-kindness, judgment, and righteousness in the earth." These three things it is certainly of the highest importance for us to know—mercy, in which alone consists all our salvation; judgment, which is executed on the wicked every day, and awaits them in a still heavier degree to eternal destruction; righteousness, by which the faithful are preserved, and most graciously supported. When you understand these things, the prophecy declares that you have abundant reason for glorying in God. Nor is this representation chargeable with an omission of his truth, or his power, or his holiness, or his goodness. For how could we have that knowledge, which is here required, of his righteousness, mercy, and judgment, unless it were supported by his inflexible veracity? And how could we believe that he governed the world in judgment and justice, if we were ignorant of his power? And whence proceeds his mercy, but from his goodness? If all his ways, then, are mercy, judgment, and righteousness, holiness also must be conspicuously displayed in them. Moreover, the knowledge of God, which is afforded us in the Scriptures, is designed for the same end as that which we derive from the creatures: it invites us first to the fear of God, and then to confidence in him; that we may learn to honour him with perfect innocence of life, and sincere obedience to his will, and to place all our dependence on his goodness.

III. But here I intend to comprise a summary of the general doctrine. And, first, let the reader observe, that the Scripture, in order to direct us to the true God, expressly excludes and rejects all the gods of the heathen; because, in almost all ages, religion has been generally corrupted. It is true, indeed, that the name of one supreme God has been universally known and celebrated. For those who used to worship a multitude of deities, whenever they spake according to the genuine sense of nature, used simply the name of God, in the singular number, as though they were contented with one God. And this was wisely remarked by Justin Martyr, who for this purpose wrote a book *On the Monarchy of God*, in which he demonstrates, from numerous testimonies, that the unity of God was a principle universally impressed on the hearts of men. Tertullian also proves the same point from the common phraseology. But since all men, without exception, have by their own vanity been drawn into erroneous notions, and so their understandings have become vain, all their natural perception of the Divine unity has only served to render them inexcusable. For even the wisest of them evidently betray the vagrant uncertainty of their minds, when they wish for some god to assist them, and in their vows call upon unknown and fabulous deities. Besides, in imagining the existence of many natures in God, though they did not entertain such absurd notions as the ignorant vulgar concerning Jupiter, Mercury, Venus, Minerva, and the rest, they were themselves by no means exempt from the delusions of Satan; and, as we have already remarked, whatever subterfuges their ingenuity has invented, none of the philosophers can exculpate themselves from the crime of revolting from God by the corruption of his truth. For this reason Habakkuk, after condemning all idols, bids us to seek "the Lord in his holy temple," that the faithful might acknowledge no other God than Jehovah, who had revealed himself in his word.

3.

Unlawfulness of Ascribing to God a Visible Form. All Idolatry a Defection from the True God.

Now, as the Scripture, in consideration of the ignorance and dulness of the human understanding, generally speaks in the plainest manner, —where it intends to discriminate between the true God and all false gods, it principally contrasts him with idols; not that it may sanction the more ingenious and plausible systems of the philosophers, but that it may better detect the folly and even madness of the world in researches concerning God, as long as everyone adheres to his own speculations. That exclusive definition, therefore, which everywhere occurs, reduces to nothing whatever notions of the Deity men may form in their own imaginations; since God alone is a sufficient witness concerning himself. In the meantime, since the whole world has been seized with such brutal stupidity, as to be desirous of visible representations of the Deity, and thus to fabricate gods of wood, stone, gold, silver, and other inanimate and corruptible materials, we ought to hold this as a certain principle, that, whenever any image is made as a representation of God, the Divine glory is corrupted by an impious falsehood. Therefore God, in the law, after having asserted the glory of Deity to belong exclusively to himself, when he intends to show what worship he approves or rejects, immediately adds, "Thou shalt not make unto thee any graven image, or any likeness." In these words he forbids us to attempt a representation of him in any visible figure; and briefly enumerates all the forms by which superstition had already begun to change his truth into a lie. For the Persians, we know, worshipped the sun; and the foolish heathen made for themselves as many gods as they saw stars in the heavens. There was scarcely an animal, indeed, which the Egyptians did not consider as an image of God. The Greeks appeared wiser than the rest, because they worshipped the Deity under the human form. But God compares not idols with each other, as though one were better or worse than another; but rejects, without a single exception, all statues, pictures, and other figures, in which idolaters imagined that he would be near them.

II. This it is easy to infer from the reasons which he annexes to the prohibition. First, in the writings of Moses: "Take ye therefore good heed unto yourselves; for ye saw no manner of similitude, on the day that the Lord spake unto you in Horeb, out of the midst of the fire: ye heard the voice of the words, but saw no similitude; lest ye corrupt yourselves, and make you a graven image, the similitude of any figure," &c. We see how expressly God opposes his "voice" to every "manner of similitude," to show, that whoever desires visible representations of him, is guilty of departing from him. It will be sufficient to refer to one of the Prophets, Isaiah, who insists more than all the others on this argument, that the Divine Majesty is dishonored by mean and absurd fiction, when he that is incorporeal is likened to a corporeal form; he that is invisible, to a visible image; he that is a spirit, to inanimate matter; and he that fills immensity, to a log of wood, a small stone, or a lump of gold. Paul also reasons in the same manner: "Forasmuch, then, as we are the offspring of God, we ought not to think that the Godhead is like unto gold, or silver, or stone, graven by art and man's device."

Whence it follows, that whatever statues are erected, or images painted, to represent God, they are only displeasing to him, as being so many insults to the Divine Majesty. And why should we wonder at the Holy Spirit thundering forth such oracles from heaven, since he compels the blind and wretched idolaters to make a similar confession on earth? Well known is the complaint of Seneca, which is cited by Augustine: "They dedicate (says he) the vilest and meanest materials to represent the sacred, immortal, and inviolable gods; and give them some a human form, and some a brutal one, and some a double sex, and different bodies; and they confer the name of gods upon images which, if animated, would be accounted monsters." Hence it further appears that the pretence set up by the advocates for idols, that they were forbidden to the Jews because they were prone to superstition, is only a frivolous cavil, to evade the force of the argument. As if truly that were peculiarly applicable to one nation, which God deduces from his eternal existence, and the invariable order of nature! Besides, Paul was not addressing the Jews, but the Athenians, when he refuted the error of making any similitude of God.

III. Sometimes indeed God hath discovered his presence by certain signs, so that he was said to be seen "face to face;" but all the signs which he ever adopted, were well calculated for the instruction of men, and afforded clear intimations of his incomprehensible essence. For "the cloud, and the smoke, and the flame," though they were symbols of celestial glory, nevertheless operated as a restraint on the minds of all, to prevent their attempting to penetrate any further. Wherefore even Moses (to whom he manifested himself more familiarly than to any other) obtained not by his prayers a sight of the face of God, but received this answer: "Thou canst not see my face; for there shall no man see my face and live." The Holy Spirit once appeared in the form of a dove; but, as he presently disappeared again, who does not perceive that by this momentary symbol the faithful are taught that they should believe the Spirit to be invisible? that, being content with his power and grace, they might make no external representation of him. The appearances of God in the human form were preludes to his future manifestation in Christ. Therefore the Jews were not permitted to make this a pretext for erecting a symbol of Deity in the figure of a man. "The mercy seat" also, from which, under the law, God displayed the presence of his power, was so constructed, as to suggest that the best contemplation of the Divine Being is when the mind is transported beyond itself with admiration. For "the cherubim" covered it with their extended wings; the veil was spread before it; and the place itself was sufficiently concealed by its secluded situation. It is manifestly unreasonable therefore to endeavour to defend images of God and of the saints, by the example of those cherubim. For, pray, what was signified by those little images but that images are not calculated to represent the Divine mysteries? since they were formed in such a manner as, by veiling the mercy seat with their wings, to prevent not only the eyes, but all the human senses, from prying into God, and so to restrain all temerity. Moreover, the Prophet describes the seraphim whom he saw in a vision, as having "their faces covered;" to signify, that the splendour of the Divine glory is so great, that even the angels themselves cannot steadfastly behold it; and the faint sparks of it, which shine in the angels, are concealed from our view. The cherubim, however, of which we are now speaking, are acknowledged by all persons of sound judgment to have been peculiar to the old state of tutelage under the legal dispensation. To adduce them, therefore, as examples for the imitation of the present age, is quite absurd. For that puerile period, as I may call it, for which such rudiments were appointed, is now past. And, indeed, it is a shameful consideration, that heathen writers are more expert interpreters of the Divine law than the papists. Juvenal reproaches and ridicules the Jews for worshipping the white clouds and Deity of heaven. This language, indeed, is perverse and impious; but in denying that there was any image of God among them, he speaks with more truth than the papists, who idly pretend that there was some visible figure of him. But as that nation frequently broke out into idolatry, with great and sudden impetuosity, resembling the violent ebullition of water from a large spring, hence let us learn the strong propensity of the human mind to idolatry, lest, imputing to the Jews a crime common to all, we should be fascinated by the allurements of sin, and sleep the sleep of death.

IV. To the same purpose is that passage, "The idols of the heathen are silver and gold, the work of men's hands;" for the Prophet concludes, from the very materials, that they are no gods, whose images are made of gold or of silver; and takes it for granted, that every conception we form of the Deity, merely from our own understandings, is a foolish imagination. He mentions gold and silver rather than clay or stone, that the splendour or the value of the materials may procure no reverence for the idols. But he concludes in general, that nothing is more improbable, than that gods should be manufactured from any inanimate matter. At the same time he insists equally on another point—that it is presumption and madness in mortal men, who are every moment in danger of losing the fleeting breath which they draw, to dare to confer upon idols the honour due to God. Man is constrained to confess that he is a creature of a day, and yet he will have a piece of metal to be worshipped as a god, of the deity of which he is the author; for whence did idols originate, but in the will of men? There is much propriety in that sarcasm of a heathen poet, who represents one of their idols as saying, "Formerly, I was the trunk of a wild fig-tree, a useless log; when the artificer, after hesitating whether he would make me a stool or a deity, at length determined that I should be a god."

A poor mortal, forsooth, who is, as it were, expiring almost every moment, will, by his workmanship, transfer to a dead stock the name and honour of God. But as that Epicurean, in his satirical effusions, has paid no respect to any religion,—leaving this sarcasm, and others of the same kind, we should be stung and penetrated by the rebuke which the Prophet has given to the extreme stupidity of those, who, with the same wood, make a fire to warm themselves, heat an oven for baking bread, roast or boil their meat, and fabricate a god, before which they prostrate themselves, to address their humble supplications. In another place, therefore, he not only pronounces them transgressors of the law, but reproaches them for not having learned from the foundations of the earth; since, in reality, there is nothing more unreasonable than the thought of contracting the infinite and incomprehensible God within the compass of five feet. And yet this monstrous abomination, which is manifestly repugnant to the order of nature, experience demonstrates to be natural to man. It must be further observed, that idols are frequently stigmatized as being the works of men's hands, unsanctioned by Divine authority; in order to establish this principle, that all modes of worship which are merely of human invention, are detestable. The Psalmist aggravates this madness, forasmuch as men implore the aid of dead and insensible things, who are imbued with understanding to know that all things are directed solely by the power of God. But since the corruption of nature carries all nations in general, and each individual in particular, to such an excess of frenzy, the Spirit at length thunders out this direful imprecation: "Let those that make them be like unto them and every one that trusteth in them." Let it be observed, that all similitudes are equally as much forbidden as graven images; which refutes the foolish subterfuge of the Greeks; for they think themselves quite safe, if they make no sculpture of Deity, while in pictures they indulge greater liberty than any other nations. But the Lord prohibits every representation of him, whether made by the statuary, or by any other artificer, because all similitudes are criminal and insulting to the Divine Majesty.

V. I know that it is a very common observation, that images are the books of the illiterate. Gregory said so; but very different is the decision of the Spirit of God, in whose school had Gregory been taught, he would never have made such an assertion. For, since Jeremiah pronounces that "the stock is a doctrine of vanities," since Habakkuk represents "a molten image" as "a teacher of lies,"—certainly the general doctrine to be gathered from these passages is, that whatever men learn respecting God from images is equally frivolous and false. If any one object, that the Prophets only reprehended those who abuse images to the impious purposes of superstition,—that indeed I grant; but affirm also, what is evident to every one, that they utterly condemn what is assumed by the papists as an indubitable axiom, that images are substitutes for books. For they contrast images with the true God, as contraries, which can never agree. This comparison, I say, is laid down in those passages which I have just cited; that, since there is only one true God, whom the Jews worshipped, there can be no visible figures made, to serve as representations of the Divine Being, without falsehood and criminality; and all who seek the knowledge of God from such figures are under a miserable delusion. Were it not true, that all knowledge of God, sought from images, is corrupt and fallacious, it would not be so uniformly condemned by the Prophets. This at least must be granted to us, that, when we maintain the vanity and fallaciousness of the attempts of men to make visible representations of God, we do no other than recite the express declarations of the Prophets.

VI. Read likewise what has been written on this subject by Lactantius and Eusebius, who hesitate not to assume as a certainty, that all those whose images are to be seen, were mortal men. Augustine also confidently asserts the unlawfulness, not only of worshipping images, but even of erecting any with reference to God. Nor does he advance any thing different from what had, many years before, been decreed by the Elibertine council, the thirty-sixth chapter of which is as follows: "It hath been decreed, that no pictures be had in the churches, and that what is worshipped or adored be not painted on the walls." But most remarkable is what Augustine elsewhere cites from Varro, and to the truth of which he subscribes—"That they who first introduced images of the gods, removed fear and added error." If this had been a mere assertion of Varro alone, it might have perhaps but little authority; yet it should justly fill us with shame, that a heathen, groping as it were in the dark, attained so much light as to perceive that corporeal representations were unworthy of the Divine Majesty, being calculated to diminish the fear of God, and to increase error among mankind. The fact itself demonstrates this to have been spoken with equal truth and wisdom; but Augustine, having borrowed it from Varro, advances it as his own opinion. And first he observes that the most ancient errors concerning God, in which men were involved, did not originate from images, but were increased by them, as by the superaddition of new materials. He next explains that the fear of God is thereby diminished, and even destroyed; since the foolish, ridiculous, and absurd fabrication of idols would easily bring his Divinity into contempt. Of the truth of this second remark, I sincerely wish that we had not such proofs in our own experience. Whoever, therefore, desires to be rightly instructed, he must learn from some other quarter than from images, what is to be known concerning God.

VII. If the papists have any shame, let them no longer use this subterfuge, that images are the books of the illiterate; which is so clearly refuted by numerous testimonies from Scripture. Yet, though I should concede this point to them, it would avail them but little in defence of their idols. What monsters they obtrude in the place of Deity is well known. But what they call the pictures or statues of their saints—what are they but examples of the most abandoned luxury and obscenity? which if any one were desirous of imitating, he would deserve corporal punishment. Even prostitutes in brothels are to be seen in more chaste and modest attire, than those images in their temples, which they wish to be accounted images of virgins. Nor do they clothe the martyrs in habits at all more becoming. Let them adorn their idols, then, with some small degree of modesty, that the pretence of their being books of some holiness, if not less false, may be less impudent. But even then, we will reply, that this is not the method to be adopted in sacred places for the instruction of the faithful, whom God will have taught a very different doctrine from any that can be learned from such insignificant trifles. He hath commanded one common doctrine to be there proposed to all, in the preaching of his word, and in his sacred mysteries; to which they betray great inattention of mind, who are carried about by their eyes to the contemplation of idols. Whom, then, do the papists call illiterate, whose ignorance will suffer them to be taught only by images? Those, truly, whom the Lord acknowledges as his disciples; whom he honours with the revelation of his heavenly philosophy; whom he will have instructed in the healthful mysteries of his kingdom. I confess, indeed, as things are now circumstanced, that there are at present not a few who cannot bear to be deprived of such books. But whence arises this stupidity, but from being defrauded of that teaching which alone is adapted to their instruction? In fact, those who presided over the churches, resigned to idols the office of teaching, for no other reason but because they were themselves dumb. Paul testifies, that in the true preaching of this gospel, Christ is "evidently set forth," and, as it were, "crucified before our eyes." To what purpose, then, was the erection of so many crosses of wood and stone, silver and gold, every where in the temples, if it had been fully and faithfully inculcated, that Christ died that he might bear our curse on the cross, expiate our sins by the sacrifice of his body, cleanse us by his blood, and, in a word, reconcile us to God the Father? From this simple declaration they might learn more than from a thousand crosses of wood or stone; for perhaps the avaricious fix their minds and their eyes more tenaciously on the gold and silver crosses, than on any part of the Divine word.

VIII. Respecting the origin of idols, the generally received opinion agrees with what is asserted in the book of Wisdom; namely, that the first authors of them were persons who paid this honour to the dead, from a superstitious reverence for their memory. I grant that this perverse custom was very ancient, and deny not that it greatly contributed to increase the rage of mankind after idolatry; nevertheless, I cannot concede that it was the first cause of that evil. For it appears from Moses, that idols were in use long before the introduction of that ostentatious consecration of the images of the dead, which is frequently mentioned by profane writers. When he relates that Rachel stole her father's idols, he speaks as of a common corruption. Whence we may infer, that the mind of man is, if I may be allowed the expression, a perpetual manufactory of idols. After the deluge, there was, as it were, a regeneration of the world; but not many years elapsed before men fabricated gods according to their own fancy. And it is probable, that while the holy patriarch was yet alive, his posterity were addicted to idolatry, so that, with the bitterest grief, he might, with his own eyes, behold the earth which God had lately purged from its corruptions by such a dreadful judgment, again polluted with idols. For Terah and Nachor, before the birth of Abraham, were worshippers of false gods, as is asserted by Joshua. Since the posterity of Shem so speedily degenerated, what opinion must we entertain of the descendants of Ham, who had already been cursed in their father? The true state of the case is, that the mind of man, being full of pride and temerity, dares to conceive of God according to its own standard; and, being sunk in stupidity, and immersed in profound ignorance; imagines a vain and ridiculous phantom instead of God. These evils are followed by another; men attempt to express in the work of their hands such a deity as they have imagined in their minds. The mind then begets the idol, and the hand brings it forth. The example of the Israelites proves this to have been the origin of idolatry, namely, that men believe not God to be among them, unless he exhibit some external signs of his presence. "As for this Moses," they said, "we wot not what is become of him; make us gods which shall go before us." They knew, indeed, that there was a God, whose power they had experienced in so many miracles; but they had no confidence in his being present with them, unless they could see some corporeal symbol of his countenance, as a testimony of their Divine Guide. They wished, therefore, to understand, from the image going before them, that God was the leader of their march. Daily experience teaches, that the flesh is never satisfied, till it has obtained some image, resembling itself, in which it may be foolishly gratified, as an image of God. In almost all ages, from the creation of the world, in obedience to this stupid propensity, men have erected visible representations, in which they believed God to be presented to their carnal eyes.

IX. Such an invention is immediately attended with adoration; for when men supposed that they saw God in images, they also worshipped him in them. At length, both their eyes and their minds being wholly confined to them, they began to grow more stupid, and to admire them, as though they possessed some inherent divinity. Now, it is plain that men did not rush into the worship of images, till they had imbibed some very gross opinion respecting them; not, indeed, that they believed them to be gods, but they imagined that something of Divinity resided in them. When you prostrate yourself, therefore, in adoration of an image, whether you suppose it to represent God or a creature, you are already fascinated with superstition. For this reason the Lord hath prohibited, not only the erection of statues made as representations of him, but also the consecration of any inscriptions or monuments to stand as objects of worship. For the same reason, also, another point is annexed to the precept in the law concerning adoration. For as soon as men have made a visible figure of God, they attach Divine power to it. Such is the stupidity of men, that they confine God to any image which they make to represent him, and therefore cannot but worship it. Nor is it of any importance, whether they worship simply the idol, or God in the idol; it is always idolatry, when

Divine honours are paid to an idol, under any pretence whatsoever. And as God will not be worshipped in a superstitious or idolatrous manner, whatever is conferred on idols is taken from him. Let this be considered by those who seek such miserable pretexts for the defence of that execrable idolatry, with which, for many ages, true religion has been overwhelmed and subverted. The images, they say, are not considered as gods. Neither were the Jews so thoughtless as not to remember, that it was God by whose hand they had been conducted out of Egypt, before they made the calf. But when Aaron said that those were the gods by whom they had been liberated from Egypt, they boldly assented; signifying, doubtless, that they would keep in remembrance, that God himself was their deliverer, while they could see him going before them in the calf. Nor can we believe the heathen to have been so stupid, as to conceive that God was no other than wood and stone. For they changed the images at pleasure, but always retained in their minds the same gods; and there were many images for one god; nor did they imagine to themselves gods in proportion to the multitude of images: besides, they daily consecrated new images, but without supposing that they made new gods. Read the excuses, which, Augustine says, were alleged by the idolaters of the age in which he lived. When they were charged with idolatry, the vulgar replied, that they worshipped, not the visible figure, but the Divinity that invisibly dwelt in it. But they, whose religion was, as he expresses himself, more refined, said, that they worshipped neither the image, nor the spirit represented by it; but that in the corporeal figure they beheld a sign of that which they ought to worship. What is to be inferred from this, but that all idolaters, whether Jewish or Gentile, have been guided by the notion which I have mentioned? Not content with a spiritual knowledge of God, they thought that they should receive more clear and familiar impressions of him by means of images. After they had once pleased themselves with such a preposterous representation of God, they ceased not from being deluded with new fallacies, till they imagined that God displayed his power in images. Nevertheless, the Jews were persuaded that, under such images, they worshipped the eternal God, the one true Lord of heaven and earth; and the heathen, that they worshipped their false gods, whom they pretended to be inhabitants of heaven.

X. Those who deny that this has been done in time past, and even within our own remembrance, assert an impudent falsehood. For why do they prostrate themselves before images? And when about to pray, why do they turn themselves towards them, as towards the ears of God? For it is true, as Augustine says, “That no man prays or worships thus, looking on an image, who is not impressed with an opinion that he shall be heard by it, and a hope that it will do for him as he desires.” Why is there so great a difference between images of the same god, that one is passed by with little or no respect, and another is honoured in the most solemn manner? Why do they fatigue themselves with votive pilgrimages, in going to see images resembling those which they have at home? Why do they at this day fight, even to slaughter and destruction, in defence of them, as of their country and religion, so that they could part with the only true God more easily than with their idols? Yet I am not here enumerating the gross errors of the vulgar, which are almost infinite, and occupy nearly the hearts of all; I only relate what they themselves allege, when they are most anxious to exculpate themselves from idolatry. “We never,” say they, “call them our gods.” Nor did the Jews or heathen in ancient times call them their gods; and yet the Prophets, in all their writings, were constantly accusing them of fornication with wood and stone, only on account of such things as are daily practised by those who wish to be thought Christians; that is, for worshipping God, by corporeal adoration before figures of wood or stone.

XI. I am neither ignorant, nor desirous of concealing, that they evade the charge by a more subtle distinction, which will soon be noticed more at large. They pretend that the reverence which they pay to images is ειδωλοδουλεια, (service of images,) but deny that it is ειδωλολατρεια (worship of images.) For in this manner they express themselves, when they maintain, that the reverence which they call *dulia*, may be given to statues or pictures, without injury to God. They consider themselves, therefore, liable to no blame, while they are only the servants of their idols, and not worshippers of them; as though worship were not rather inferior to service. And yet, while they seek to shelter themselves under a Greek term, they contradict themselves in the most childish manner. For since the Greek word λατρευειν signifies nothing else but to worship, what they say is equivalent to a confession that they adore their images, but without adoration. Nor can they justly object, that I am trying to insnare them with words: they betray their own ignorance in their endeavours to raise a mist before the eyes of the simple. But, however eloquent they may be, they will never be able, by their rhetoric, to prove one and the same thing to be two different things. Let them point out, I say, a difference in fact, that they may be accounted different from ancient idolaters. For as an adulterer, or homicide, will not escape the imputation of guilt, by giving his crime a new and arbitrary name, so it is absurd that these persons should be exculpated by the subtle invention of a name, if they really differ in no respect from those idolaters whom they themselves are constrained to condemn. But their case is so far from being different from that of former idolaters, that the source of all the evil is a preposterous emulation, with which they have rivalled them by exercising their minds in contriving, and their hands in forming, visible symbols of the Deity.

XII. Nevertheless, I am not so scrupulous as to think that no images ought ever to be permitted. But since sculpture and painting are gifts of God, I wish for a pure and legitimate use of both; lest those things, which the Lord hath conferred on us for his glory and our benefit, be not only corrupted by preposterous abuse, but even perverted to our ruin. We think it unlawful to make any visible figure as a representation of God, because he hath himself forbidden it, and it cannot be done without detracting, in some measure, from his glory. Let it not be supposed that we are singular in this opinion; for that all sound writers have uniformly reprobated the practice, must be evident to persons conversant with their works. If, then, it be not lawful to make any corporeal representation of God, much less will it be lawful to worship it for God, or to worship God in it. We conclude, therefore, that nothing should be painted and engraved but objects visible to our eyes: the Divine Majesty, which is far above the reach of human sight, ought not to be corrupted by unseemly figures. The subjects of those arts consist partly of histories and transactions, partly of images and corporeal forms, without reference to any transactions. The former are of some use in information or recollection; the latter, as far as I see, can furnish nothing but amusement. And yet it is evident, that almost all the images, which have hitherto been set up in the churches, have been of this latter description. Hence it may be seen, that they were placed there, not with judgment and discrimination, but from a foolish and inconsiderate passion for them. I say nothing here of the impropriety and indecency conspicuous in most of them, and the wanton licentiousness displayed in them by the painters and statuaries, at which I have before hinted: I only assert, that even if they were intrinsically faultless, still they would be altogether unavailing for the purposes of instruction.

XIII. But, passing over that difference also, let us consider, as we proceed, whether it be expedient to have any images at all in Christian temples, either descriptive of historical events, or representative of human forms. In the first place, if the authority of the ancient Church have any influence with us, let us remember, that for about five hundred years, while religion continued in a more prosperous state, and purer doctrine prevailed, the Christian churches were generally without images. They were then first introduced, therefore, to ornament the churches, when the purity of the ministry had begun to degenerate. I will not dispute what was the reason which influenced the first authors of them; but if you compare one age with another, you will see that they were much declined from the integrity of those who had no images. Who can suppose, that those holy fathers would have permitted the Church to remain so long destitute of what they judged useful and salutary for it? The fact was, that, instead of omitting them through ignorance or negligence, they perceived them to be of little or no use, but, on the contrary, pregnant with much danger; and, therefore, intentionally and wisely rejected them. This is asserted in express terms by Augustine: "When they are fixed," says he, "in those places in an honourable elevation, to attract the attention of those who are praying and sacrificing, though they are destitute of sense and life, yet, by the very similitude of living members and senses, they affect weak minds, so that they appear to them to live and breathe," &c. And in another place: "For that representation of members leads, and, as it were, constrains, the mind, which animates a body, to suppose that body to be endued with perception, which it sees to be very similar to its own," &c. And a little after: "Idols have more influence to bow down an unhappy soul, because they have a mouth, eyes, ears, and feet, than to correct it, because they neither speak, nor see, nor hear, nor walk." This indeed appears to be the reason of John's exhortation to "keep ourselves," not only from the worship of idols, but "from idols" themselves. And we have found it too true, that, through the horrible frenzy, which, almost to the total destruction of piety, hath heretofore possessed the world, as soon as images are set up in churches, there is, as it were, a standard of idolatry erected; for the folly of mankind cannot refrain from immediately falling into idolatrous worship. But, even if the danger were less, yet, when I consider the use for which temples were designed, it appears to me extremely unworthy of their sanctity, to receive any other images, than those natural and expressive ones, which the Lord hath consecrated in his word; I mean Baptism, and the Supper of the Lord, and the other ceremonies, with which our eyes ought to be more attentively engaged, and more sensibly affected, than to require any others formed by human ingenuity. Behold the incomparable advantages of images! the loss of which, if you believe the papists, nothing can compensate.

XIV. The remarks already made on this subject, I think, would be sufficient, if it were not necessary to take some notice of the Council of Nice; not that very celebrated one, which was convened by Constantine the Great, but that which was held about eight hundred years ago, by the command, and under the auspices, of the Empress Irene. For that Council decreed, not only that images should be had in churches, but also that they should be worshipped. And, notwithstanding what I have advanced, the authority of the Council would raise a strong prejudice on the contrary side. Though, to confess the truth, I am not much concerned at this, as I am to show the reader their extreme madness, whose fondness for images exceeded any thing that was becoming in Christians. But let us despatch this point first: the present advocates for the use of images, allege the authority of that Nicene Council in their defence. There is a book extant, written in refutation of this practice, under the name of Charlemagne; which, from the diction, we may conclude was composed at the same time. In this work are recited the opinions of the bishops who attended the Council, and the arguments they used in the controversy. John, the delegate of the Eastern churches, said, "God created man in his own image;" and hence he inferred that we ought to have images. The same prelate thought that images were recommended to us by this sentence: "Show me thy face, for it is glorious." Another, to prove that they ought to be placed on the altars, cited this testimony: "No man lighteth a candle, and putteth it under a bushel." Another, to show the contemplation of these to be useful to us, adduced a verse from a Psalm: "The light of thy countenance, O Lord, is sealed upon us." Another pressed this comparison into his service: "As the patriarchs used the sacrifices of the heathen, so Christians ought to have the images of saints, instead of the idols of the heathen." In the same manner they tortured that expression, "Lord, I have loved the beauty of thy house." But the most ingenious of all was their interpretation of this passage: "As we have heard, so have we seen;" that therefore God is known, not only by the hearing of his word, but by the contemplation of images. Similar is the subtlety of Bishop Theodore: "God is glorious in his saints." And in another place it is said, "In the saints that are in the earth:" therefore this ought to be referred to images. But their impertinencies and absurdities are so disgusting, that I am quite ashamed to repeat them.

XV. When they dispute concerning adoration, they bring forward Jacob's worshipping of Pharaoh, and of the staff of Joseph, and of the inscription erected by himself; although, in this last instance, they not only corrupt the sense of the Scripture, but allege what is nowhere to be found. These passages also, "Worship his footstool;" "Worship in his holy hill;" and, "All the rich of the people shall supplicate thy face;" they consider as apposite and conclusive proofs. If any one wished to represent the advocates for images in a ridiculous point of view, could he possibly ascribe to them greater and grosser instances of folly? But, that no doubt of this might remain, Theodosius, bishop of Mira, defends the propriety of worshipping images from the dreams of his archdeacon, as seriously as if he had an immediate revelation from heaven. Now, let the advocates of images go and urge upon us the decree of that Council; as though those venerable fathers had not entirely destroyed all their credit by such puerile treatment of the sacred Scriptures, or such impious and shameful mutilation of them.

XVI. I come now to those prodigies of impiety, which it is wonderful that they ever ventured to broach; and more wonderful still, that they have not been opposed with universal detestation. It is right to expose this flagitious madness, that the worship of images may at least be deprived of the pretence of antiquity, which the papists falsely urge in its favour. Theodosius, bishop of Amorum, denounces an anathema against all who are averse to the worship of images. Another imputes all the calamities of Greece and the East to the crime of not having worshipped them. What punishments, then, did the Prophets, Apostles, and Martyrs deserve, in whose time images were unknown? They add further, If the image of the emperor be met by processions with perfumes and incense, much more is this honour due to the images of the saints. Constantius, bishop of Constance, in Cyprus, professes his reverence for images, and avows that he will pay them the same worship and honour as is due to the Trinity, the source of all life; and whoever refuses to do the same, he anathematizes and dismisses with the Manichees and Marcionites. And, lest you should suppose this to be the private opinion of an individual, they all declare their assent to it. John, the delegate of the Eastern churches, carried by the fervour of his zeal to still greater lengths, asserts it to be better to admit all the brothels of the world into one city, than to reject the worship of images. At length it was unanimously decreed, that the Samaritans were worse than all heretics, and that the adversaries of images were worse than the Samaritans. But, that the farce might not want its usual plaudit, they add this clause: "Let them rejoice and exult, who have the image of Christ, and offer sacrifice to it." Where is now the distinction of *latria* and *dulia*, with which they attempt to deceive both God and men? For the Council gives the same honour, without any exception, to images and to the living God.

4.

God Contradistinguished from Idols, that He May Be Solely and Supremely Worshipped.

We said, at the beginning, that the knowledge of God consists not in frigid speculation, but is accompanied by the worship of him. We also cursorily touched on the right method of worshipping him, which will be more fully explained in other places. I now only repeat, in few words, that whenever the Scripture asserts that there is but one God, it contends not for the bare name, but also teaches, that whatever belongs to the Deity, should not be transferred to another. This shows how pure religion differs from idolatry. The Greek word ευσεβεια certainly signifies right worship, since even blind mortals, groping in the dark, have always perceived the necessity of some certain rule, that the worship of God may not be involved in disorder and confusion. Although Cicero ingeniously and correctly derives the word *religion* from a verb signifying "to read over again," or "to gather again;" yet the reason he assigns for it, that good worshippers often recollect, and diligently reconsider what is true, is forced and far-fetched. I rather think the word is opposed to a liberty of wandering without restraint; because the greater part of the world rashly embraces whatever they meet with, and also ramble from one thing to another; but piety, in order to walk with a steady step, collects itself within its proper limits. The word *superstition* also appears to me to import a discontent with the method and order prescribed, and an accumulation of a superfluous mass of vain things. But to leave the consideration of words, it has been generally admitted, in all ages, that religion is corrupted and perverted by errors and falsehoods; whence we infer, that when we allow ourselves anything from inconsiderate zeal, the pretext alleged by the superstitious is altogether frivolous. Although this confession is in the mouths of all, they betray, at the same time, a shameful ignorance, neither adhering to the one true God, nor observing any discrimination in his worship, as we have before shown. But God, to assert his own right, proclaims that he is "jealous," and will be a severe avenger, if men confound him with any fictitious deity; and then, to retain mankind in obedience, he defines his legitimate worship. He comprises both in his law, where he first binds the faithful to himself, as their sole legislator; and then prescribes a rule for the right worship of him according to his will. Now, of the law, since the uses and ends of it are various, I shall treat in its proper place: at present, I only remark, that it sets up a barrier to prevent men turning aside to corrupt modes of worship. Let us remember, what I have already stated, that, unless every thing belonging to Divinity remain in God alone, he is spoiled of his honour, and his worship is violated. And here it is necessary to animadvert more particularly on the subtle fallacies of superstition. For it revolts not to strange gods, in such a manner as to appear to desert the supreme God, or to degrade him to a level with others; but, allowing him the highest place, it surrounds him with a multitude of inferior deities, among whom it distributes his honours; and thus, in a cunning and hypocritical manner, the glory of Divinity is divided among many, instead of remaining wholly in one. Thus the ancient idolaters, Jews as well as Gentiles, imagined one God, the Father and Governor of all, and subordinate to him a vast multitude of other deities; to whom, in common with the supreme God, they attributed the government of heaven and earth.

Thus the saints, who departed out of this life some ages ago, are exalted to the society of God, to be worshipped, and invoked, and celebrated like him. We suppose, indeed, the glory of God not to be sullied with this abomination; whereas it is, in a great measure, suppressed and extinguished, except that we retain some faint notion of his supreme power; but, at the same time, deceived with such impostures, we are seduced to the worship of various deities.

II. On this account was invented the distinction of *latria* and *dulia*, as they express themselves, by which they conceived they might safely ascribe divine honours to angels and deceased men. For it is evident, that the worship which papists pay to the saints, differs not in reality from the worship of God; for they adore God and them promiscuously; but when they are accused of it, they evade the charge with this subterfuge, that they preserve inviolate to God what belongs to him, because they leave him λατρεια. But since the question relates to a thing, not to a word, who can bear their careless trifling on the most important of all subjects? But, to pass this also, they will gain nothing at last by their distinction, but that they render worship to God alone, and service to the saints. For λατρεια, in Greek, signifies the same as *cultus* in Latin, [and *worship* in English;] but δουλεια properly signifies *servitus*, [*service*;] and yet, in the Scriptures, this distinction is sometimes disregarded. But, suppose it to be a constant distinction, it remains to be inquired, what is the meaning of each term. Λατρεια is *worship*; δουλεια is *service*. Now, no one doubts, that to serve is more than to worship or honour. For it would be irksome to serve many persons, whom you would not refuse to honour. So unjust is the distribution, to assign the greater to the saints, and leave to God that which is less. But many of the ancients, it is urged, have used this distinction. What is that to the purpose, if everyone perceives it to be not only improper, but altogether frivolous?

III. Leaving these subtleties, let us consider the subject itself. Paul, when he reminds the Galatians what they had been before they were illuminated in the knowledge of God, says, that they "did service to them which by nature were no gods." Though he mentions not λατρεια, (worship,) is their idolatry therefore excusable? He certainly condemns that perverse superstition, which he denominates δουλεια, (service,) equally as much as if he had used the word λατρεια, (worship.) And when Christ repels the assault of Satan with this shield, "It is written, Thou shalt worship the Lord thy God," the word λατρεια came not into the question; for Satan required nothing but προσκυνησις, (prostration, or adoration.) So, when John is reprehended by an angel, for having fallen on his knees before him, we must not understand that John was so stupid as to intend to transfer to an angel the honour due exclusively to God. But since all worship, that is connected with religion, cannot but savour of Divine, he could not (προσκυνειν) prostrate himself before the angel, without detracting from the glory of God. We read, indeed, frequently, of men having been worshipped; but that was civil honour, so to speak; religion has a different design; and no sooner is religion connected with worship, or homage, than it produces a profanation of the Divine honour. We may see the same in Cornelius, who had not made such a small progress in piety, as not to ascribe supreme worship to God alone. When he "fell down" before Peter, therefore, it certainly was not with an intention of worshipping him instead of God: yet Peter positively forbade him to do it. And why was this, but because men never so particularly distinguish between the worship or homage of God, and that of the creatures, as to avoid transferring to a creature what belongs exclusively to God? Wherefore, if we desire to have but one God, let us remember, that his glory ought not, in the least, to be diminished; but that he must retain all that belongs to him. Therefore Zechariah, when speaking of the restoration of the Church, expressly declares, not only that "there shall be one Lord," but also "that his name shall be one;" signifying, without doubt, that he will have nothing in common with idols. Now, what kind of worship God requires, will be seen, in due course, in another place. For he hath been pleased, in his law, to prescribe to mankind what is lawful and right; and so to confine them to a certain rule, that every individual might not take the liberty of inventing a mode of worship according to his own fancy. But, since it is not proper to burden the reader, by confounding many subjects together, I shall not enter on that point yet; let it suffice to know, that no religious services can be transferred to any other than God alone, without committing sacrilege. At first, indeed, superstition ascribed Divine honours either to the sun, or to the other stars, or to idols. Afterwards followed ambition, which, adorning men with the spoils of God, dared to profane every thing that was sacred. And although there remained a persuasion, that they ought to worship a supreme God, yet it became customary to offer sacrifices promiscuously to genii, and inferior deities, and deceased heroes. So steep is the descent to this vice, to communicate to a vast multitude that which God particularly challenges to himself alone!

5.

One Divine Essence, Containing Three Persons; Taught in the Scriptures from the Beginning.

What is taught in the Scriptures concerning the immensity and spirituality of the essence of God, should serve not only to overthrow the foolish notions of the vulgar, but also to refute the subtleties of profane philosophy. One of the ancients, in his own conception very shrewdly, said, that whatever we see, and whatever we do not see, is God. But he imagined that the Deity was diffused through every part of the world. But, although God, to keep us within the bounds of sobriety, speaks but rarely of his essence, yet, by those two attributes, which I have mentioned, he supersedes all gross imaginations, and represses the presumption of the human mind. For, surely, his immensity ought to inspire us with awe, that we may not attempt to measure him with our senses; and the spirituality of his nature prohibits us from entertaining any earthly or carnal speculations concerning him. For the same reason, he represents his residence to be "in heaven;" for though, as he is incomprehensible, he fills the earth also; yet, seeing that our minds, from their dulness, are continually dwelling on the earth, in order to shake off our sloth and inactivity, he properly raises us above the world. And here is demolished the error of the Manichees, who, by maintaining the existence of two original principles, made the devil, as it were, equal to God. This certainly was both dividing the unity of God, and limiting his immensity. For their daring to abuse certain testimonies of Scripture betrayed a shameful ignorance; as the error itself evidenced an execrable madness. The Anthropomorphites also, who imagined God to be corporeal, because the Scripture frequently ascribes to him a mouth, ears, eyes, hands, and feet, are easily refuted. For who, even of the meanest capacity, understands not, that God lisps, as it were, with us, just as nurses are accustomed to speak to infants? Wherefore, such forms of expression do not clearly explain the nature of God, but accommodate the knowledge of him to our narrow capacity; to accomplish which, the Scripture must necessarily descend far below the height of his majesty.

II. But he also designates himself by another peculiar character, by which he may be yet more clearly distinguished; for, while he declares himself to be but One, he proposes himself to be distinctly considered in Three Persons, without apprehending which, we have only a bare and empty name of God floating in our brains, without any idea of the true God. Now, that no one may vainly dream of three gods, or suppose that the simple essence of God is divided among the three Persons, we must seek for a short and easy definition, which will preserve us from all error. But since some violently object to the word Person, as of human invention, we must first examine the reasonableness of this objection. When the Apostle denominates the Son the express image of the hypostasis of the Father, he undoubtedly ascribes to the Father some subsistence, in which he differs from the Son. For to understand this word as synonymous with Essence, (as some interpreters have done, as though Christ, like wax impressed with a seal, represented in himself the substance of the Father,) were not only harsh, but also absurd. For the essence of God being simple and indivisible, he who contains all in himself, not in part, or by derivation, but in complete perfection, could not, without impropriety, and even absurdity, be called the express image of it. But since the Father, although distinguished by his own peculiar property, hath expressed himself entirely in his Son, it is with the greatest reason asserted that he hath made his hypostasis conspicuous in him; with which the other appellation, given him in the same passage, of "the brightness of his glory," exactly corresponds. From the words of the Apostle, we certainly conclude, that there is in the Father a proper hypostasis, which is conspicuous in the Son. And thence also we easily infer the hypostasis of the Son, which distinguishes him from the Father. The same reasoning is applicable to the Holy Spirit; for we shall soon prove him also to be God; and yet he must, of necessity, be considered as distinct from the Father. But this is not a distinction of the essence, which it is unlawful to represent as any other than simple and undivided. It follows, therefore, if the testimony of the Apostle be credited, that there are in God three *hypostases*. And, as the Latins have expressed the same thing by the word *person*, it is too fastidious and obstinate to contend about so clear a matter. If we wish to translate word for word, we may call it *subsistence*. Many, in the same sense, have called it *substance*. Nor has the word *person* been used by the Latins only; but the Greeks also, for the sake of testifying their consent to this doctrine, taught the existence of three προσωπα (persons) in God. But both Greeks and Latins, notwithstanding any verbal difference, are in perfect harmony respecting the doctrine itself.

III. Now, though heretics rail at the word *person*, or some morose and obstinate men clamorously refuse to admit a name of human invention; since they cannot make us assert that there are three, each of whom is entirely God, nor yet that there are more gods than one, how very unreasonable is it to reprobate words which express nothing but what is testified and recorded in the Scriptures! It were better, say they, to restrain not only our thoughts, but our expressions also, within the limits of the Scripture, than to introduce exotic words, which may generate future dissensions and disputes; for thus we weary ourselves with verbal controversies; thus the truth is lost in altercation; thus charity expires in odious contention. If they call every word exotic, which cannot be found in the Scriptures in so many syllables, they impose on us a law which is very unreasonable, and which condemns all interpretation, but what is composed of detached texts of Scripture connected together. But if by exotic they mean that which is curiously contrived, and superstitiously defended, which tends to contention more than to edification, the use of which is either unseasonable or unprofitable, which offends pious ears with its harshness, and seduces persons from the simplicity of the Divine word, I most cordially embrace their modest opinion. For I think that we ought to speak of God with the same religious caution, which should govern our thoughts of him; since all the thoughts that we entertain concerning him merely from ourselves, are foolish, and all our expressions absurd. But there is a proper medium to be observed: we should seek in the Scriptures a certain rule, both for thinking and for speaking; by which we may regulate all the thoughts of our minds, and all the words of our mouths. But what forbids our expressing, in plainer words, those things which, in the Scriptures, are, to our understanding, intricate and obscure, provided our expressions religiously and faithfully convey the true sense of the Scripture, and are used with modest caution, and not without sufficient occasion? Of this, examples sufficiently numerous are not wanting. But, when it shall have been proved, that the Church was absolutely necessitated to use the terms Trinity and Persons, if any one then censures the novelty of the words, may he not be justly considered as offended at the light of the truth? as having no other cause of censure, but that the truth is explained and elucidated?

IV. But such verbal novelty (if it must have this appellation) is principally used, when the truth is to be asserted in opposition to malicious cavillers, who elude it by crafty evasions; of which we have too much experience in the present day, who find great difficulty in refuting the enemies of pure and sound doctrine: possessed of serpentine lubricity, they escape by the most artful expedients, unless they are vigorously pursued, and held fast when once caught. Thus the ancients, pestered with various controversies against erroneous dogmas, were constrained to express their sentiments with the utmost perspicuity, that they might leave no subterfuges to the impious, who availed themselves of obscure expressions, for the concealment of their errors. Unable to resist the clear testimonies of the Scriptures, Arius confessed Christ to be God, and the Son of God; and, as though this were all that was necessary, he pretended to agree with the Church at large. But, at the same time, he continued to maintain that Christ was created, and had a beginning like other creatures. To draw the versatile subtlety of this man from its concealment, the ancient Fathers proceeded further, and declared Christ to be the eternal Son of the Father, and consubstantial with the Father. Here impiety openly discovered itself, when the Arians began inveterately to hate and execrate the name ὁμοούσιος, (consubstantial.) But if, in the first instance, they had sincerely and cordially confessed Christ to be God, they would not have denied him to be consubstantial with the Father. Who can dare to censure those good men, as quarrelsome and contentious, for having kindled such a flame of controversy, and disturbed the peace of the Church on account of one little word? That little word distinguished Christians, who held the pure faith, from sacrilegious Arians. Afterwards arose Sabellius, who considered the names of Father, Son, and Holy Spirit, as little more than empty sounds; arguing, that they were not used on account of any real distinction, but were different attributes of God, whose attributes of this kind are numerous. If the point came to be controverted, he confessed, that he believed the Father to be God, the Son God, and the Holy Spirit God; but he would readily evade all the force of this confession, by adding, that he had said no other than if he had called God potent, and just, and wise. And thus he came to another conclusion, that the Father is the Son, and that the Holy Spirit is the Father, without any order or distinction. The good doctors of that age, who had the interest of religion at heart, in order to counteract the wickedness of this man, maintained, on the contrary, that they ought really to acknowledge three peculiar properties in one God. And, to defend themselves against his intricate subtleties, by the plain and simple truth, they affirmed, that they truly subsisted in the one God; or, what is the same, that in the unity of God there subsisted a trinity of Persons.

V. If, then, the words have not been rashly invented, we should beware lest we be convicted of fastidious temerity in rejecting them. I could wish them, indeed, to be buried in oblivion, provided this faith were universally received, that the Father, Son, and Holy Spirit, are the one God; and that nevertheless the Son is not the Father, nor the Spirit the Son, but that they are distinguished from each other by some peculiar property. I am not so rigidly precise as to be fond of contending for mere words. For I observe that the ancients, who otherwise speak on these subjects with great piety, are not consistent with each other, nor, in all cases, with themselves. For what forms of expression, adopted by councils, does Hilary excuse! To what extremes does

Augustine sometimes proceed! How different are the Greeks from the Latins! But of this variation, let one example suffice: when the Latins would translate the word ὁμοούσιος, they called it *consubstantial*, signifying the *substance* of the Father and the Son to be one, and thus using *substance* for *essence*. Whence also Jerome, writing to Damasus, pronounces it to be sacrilege to say that there are three *substances* in God. Yet, that there are three *substances* in God, you will find asserted in Hilary more than a hundred times. But how perplexed is Jerome on the word *hypostasis*! For he suspects some latent poison in the assertion, that there are three *hypostases* in God. And if any one uses this word in a pious sense, he refrains not from calling it an improper expression; if, indeed, he was sincere in this declaration, and did not rather knowingly and wilfully endeavour to asperse, with a groundless calumny, the bishops of the East, whom he hated. He certainly discovers not much ingenuousness in affirming that, in all the profane schools, οὐσία (essence) is the same as ὑπόστασις, (hypostasis,) which the trite and common use of the words universally contradicts. More modesty and liberality are discovered by Augustine, who, though he asserts that the word *hypostasis*, in this sense, is new to Latin ears, yet leaves the Greeks their usual phraseology, and even peaceably tolerates the Latins, who had imitated their language; and the account of Socrates, in the sixth book of his Tripartite History, seems to imply, that it was by ignorant men that it had first been improperly applied to this subject. The same Hilary accuses the heretics of a great crime, in constraining him, by their wickedness, to expose to the danger of human language those things which ought to be confined within the religion of the mind; plainly avowing that this is to do things unlawful, to express things inexpressible, to assume things not conceded. A little after, he largely excuses himself for his boldness in bringing forward new terms; for, when he has used the names of nature, Father, Son, and Spirit, he immediately adds, that whatever is sought further, is beyond the signification of language, beyond the reach of our senses, beyond the conception of our understanding. And, in another place, he pronounces that happy were the bishops of Gaul, who had neither composed, nor received, nor even known, any other confession but that ancient and very simple one, which had been received in all the churches from the days of the Apostles. Very similar is the excuse of Augustine, that this word was extorted by necessity, on account of the poverty of human language on so great a subject, not for the sake of expressing what God is, but to avoid passing it over in total silence, that the Father, Son, and Spirit are three. This moderation of those holy men should teach us, not to pass such severe censures on those who are unwilling to subscribe to expressions adopted by us, provided they are not actuated by pride, perverseness, or disingenuous subtlety. But let them also, on the other hand, consider the great necessity which constrains us to use such language, that, by degrees, they may at length be accustomed to a useful phraseology. Let them also learn to beware, since we have to oppose the Arians on one side, and the Sabellians on the other, lest, while they take offence at both these parties being deprived of all opportunity of evasion, they cause some suspicion that they are themselves the disciples either of Arius or of Sabellius. Arius confesses, "that Christ is God;" but maintains also, "that he was created, and had a beginning." He acknowledges that Christ is "one with the Father;" but secretly whispers in the ears of his disciples, that he is "united to him," like the rest of the faithful, though by a singular privilege. Say that he is *consubstantial*, you tear off the mask from the hypocrite, and yet you add nothing to the Scriptures. Sabellius asserts, "that the names Father, Son, and Spirit, are expressive of no distinction in the Godhead." Say that they are three, and he will exclaim, that you are talking of "three gods." Say, "that in the one essence of God there is a trinity of Persons," and you will at once express what the Scriptures declare, and will restrain such frivolous loquacity. Now, if any persons are prevented, by such excessive scrupulousness, from admitting these terms, yet not one of them can deny, that, when the Scripture speaks of one God, it should be understood of a unity of substance; and that, when it speaks of three in one essence, it denotes the Persons in this trinity. When this is honestly confessed, we have no further concern about words. But I have found, by long and frequent experience, that those who pertinaciously contend about words, cherish some latent poison; so that it were better designedly to provoke their resentment, than to use obscure language for the sake of obtaining their favour.

VI. But, leaving the dispute about terms, I shall now enter on the discussion of the subject itself. What I denominate a Person, is a subsistence in the Divine essence, which is related to the others, and yet distinguished from them by an incommunicable property. By the word *subsistence* we mean something different from the word *essence*. For, if the *Word* were simply God, and had no peculiar property, John had been guilty of impropriety in saying that he was always *with God*. When he immediately adds, that *the Word* also *was God*, he reminds us of the unity of the essence. But because he could not be *with God*, without subsisting in the Father, hence arises that subsistence, which, although inseparably connected with the essence, has a peculiar mark, by which it is distinguished from it. Now, I say that each of the three subsistences has a relation to the others, but is distinguished from them by a peculiar property. We particularly use the word *relation*, (or *comparison*,) here, because, when mention is made simply and indefinitely of God, this name pertains no less to the Son and Spirit, than to the Father. But whenever the Father is compared with the Son, the property peculiar to each distinguishes him from the other. Thirdly, whatever is proper to each of them, I assert to be incommunicable, because whatever is ascribed to the Father as a character of distinction, cannot be applied or transferred to the Son. Nor, indeed, do I disapprove of the definition of Tertullian, if rightly understood: "That there is in God a certain distribution or economy, which makes no change in the unity of the essence."

VII. But before I proceed any further, I must prove the Deity of the Son and of the Holy Spirit; after which we shall see how they differ from each other. When the Scripture speaks of *the Word of God*, it certainly were very absurd to imagine it to be only a transient and momentary sound, emitted into the air, and coming forth from God himself; of which nature were the oracles, given to the fathers, and all the prophecies. It is rather to be understood of the eternal wisdom residing in God, whence the oracles, and all the prophecies, proceeded. For, according to the testimony of Peter, the ancient Prophets spake by the Spirit of Christ no less than the Apostles and all the succeeding ministers of the heavenly doctrine. But, as Christ had not yet been manifested, we must necessarily understand that the Word was begotten of the Father before the world began. And if the Spirit that inspired the Prophets was the Spirit of the Word, we conclude, beyond all doubt, that the Word was truly God. And this is taught by Moses, with sufficient perspicuity, in the creation of the world, in which he represents the Word as acting such a conspicuous part. For why does he relate that God, in the creation of each of his works, said, Let this or that be done, but that the unsearchable glory of God may resplendently appear in his image? Captious and loquacious men would readily evade this argument, by saying, that the *Word* imports an order or command; but the

Apostles are better interpreters, who declare, that the worlds were created by the Son, and that he "upholds all things by the word of his power." For here we see that the *Word* intends the nod or mandate of the Son, who is himself the eternal and essential Son of the Father. Nor, to the wise and sober, is there any obscurity in that passage of Solomon, where he introduces Wisdom as begotten of the Father before time began, and presiding at the creation of the world, and over all the works of God. For, to pretend that this denotes some temporary expression of the will of God, were foolish and frivolous; whereas God then intended to discover his fixed and eternal counsel, and even something more secret. To the same purpose also is that assertion of Christ, "My Father worketh hitherto, and I work." For, by affirming that, from the beginning of the world, he had continually cooperated with the Father, he makes a more explicit declaration of what had been briefly glanced at by Moses. We conclude, therefore, that God spake thus at the creation, that the Word might have his part in the work, and so that operation be common to both. But John speaks more clearly than all others, when he represents *the Word*, who from the beginning *was God with God*, as in union with the Father, the original cause of all things. For to the Word he both attributes a real and permanent essence, and assigns some peculiar property; and plainly shows how God, by speaking, created the world. Therefore, as all Divine revelations are justly entitled *the word of God*, so we ought chiefly to esteem that substantial Word the source of all revelations, who is liable to no variation, who remains with God perpetually one and the same, and who is God himself.

VIII. Here we are interrupted by some clamorous objectors, who, since they cannot openly rob him of his divinity, secretly steal from him his eternity. For they say, that the Word only began to exist, when God opened his sacred mouth in the creation of the world. But they are too inconsiderate in imagining something new in the substance of God. For, as those names of God, which relate to his external works, began to be ascribed to him after the existence of those works, as when he is called the Creator of heaven and earth, so piety neither acknowledges nor admits any name, signifying that God has found any thing new to happen to himself. For, could any thing, from any quarter, effect a change in him, it would contradict the assertion of James, that "every good gift and every perfect gift is from above, and cometh down from the Father of lights, with whom is no variableness or shadow of turning." Nothing, then, is more intolerable, than to suppose a beginning of that Word, which was always God, and afterwards the Creator of the world. But they argue, in their own apprehension most acutely, that Moses, by representing God as having then spoken for the first time, implies also, that there was no Word in him before; than which nothing is more absurd. For it is not to be concluded, because any thing begins to be manifested at a certain time, that it had no prior existence. I form a very different conclusion; that, since, in the very instant when God said, "Let there be light," the power of the Word was clearly manifested, the Word must have existed long before. But if any one inquires, how long, he will find no beginning. For he limits no certain period of time, when he himself says, "O Father, glorify thou me with thine own self, with the glory which I had with thee before the world was." Nor is this omitted by John; for, before he descends to the creation of the world, he declares that the Word "was in the beginning with God." We therefore conclude again, that the Word, conceived of God before time began, perpetually remained with him, which proves his eternity, his true essence, and his divinity.

IX. Though I advert not yet to the person of the Mediator, but defer it to that part of the work which will relate to redemption, yet, since it ought, without controversy, to be believed by all, that Christ is the very same Word clothed in flesh, any testimonies which assert the Deity of Christ, will be very properly introduced here. When it is said, in the forty-fifth Psalm, "Thy throne, O God, is for ever and ever," the Jews endeavour to evade its force, by pleading that the name Elohim is applicable also to angels, and to men of dignity and power. But there cannot be found in the Scripture a similar passage, which erects an eternal throne for a creature; for he is not merely called God, but is also declared to possess an eternal dominion. Besides, this title is never given to a creature, without some addition, as when it is said that Moses should be "a god to Pharaoh." Some read it in the genitive case, "Thy throne is of God," which is extremely insipid. I confess, indeed, that what is eminently and singularly excellent, is frequently called Divine; but it sufficiently appears from the context, that such a meaning would be uncouth and forced, and totally inapplicable here. But, if their perverseness refuse to yield this point, there certainly is no obscurity in Isaiah, where he introduces Christ as God, and as crowned with supreme power, which is the prerogative of God alone. "His name," says he, "shall be called the Mighty God, the Father of eternity," &c. Here also the Jews object, and invert the reading of the passage in this manner: "This is the name by which the mighty God, the Father of eternity, shall call him," &c.; so that they would leave the Son only the title of Prince of peace. But to what purpose would so many epithets be accumulated in this passage on God the Father, when the design of the prophet is to distinguish Christ by such eminent characters as may establish our faith in him? Wherefore, there can be no doubt that he is there denominated the Mighty God, just as, a little before, he is called Immanuel. But nothing can be required plainer than a passage in Jeremiah, that this should be the name whereby the Branch of David shall be called "Jehovah our righteousness." For since the Jews themselves teach, that all other names of God are mere epithets, but that this alone, which they call ineffable, is a proper name expressive of his Essence, we conclude, that the Son is the one eternal God, who declares, in another place, that he "will not give his glory to another." This also they endeavour to evade, because Moses imposed this name on an altar which he built, and Ezekiel on the city of the new Jerusalem. But who does not perceive, that the altar was erected as a monument of Moses having been exalted by God, and that Jerusalem is honoured with the name of God, only as a testimony of the Divine presence? For thus speaks the prophet: "The name of the city shall be, Jehovah is there." But Moses expresses himself thus: He "built an altar, and called the name of it Jehovah-nissi," (my exaltation.) But there is more contention about another passage of Jeremiah, where the same title is given to Jerusalem in these words: "This is the name wherewith she shall be called, Jehovah our righteousness." But this testimony is so far from opposing the truth which we are defending, that it rather confirms it. For, having before testified that Christ is the true Jehovah, from whom righteousness proceeds, he now pronounces that the church will have such a clear apprehension of it, as to be able to glory in the same name. In the former place, then, is shown the original cause of righteousness, in the latter the effect.

X. Now, if these things do not satisfy the Jews, I see not by what cavils they can evade the accounts of Jehovah having so frequently appeared in the character of an angel. An angel is said to have appeared to the holy fathers. He claims for himself the name of the eternal God. If it be objected, that this is spoken with regard to the character which he sustains, this by no means removes the difficulty. For a servant would never rob God of his honour, by permitting sacrifice to be offered to himself. But the angel, refusing to eat bread, commands a sacrifice to be offered to Jehovah. He afterwards demonstrates that he is really Jehovah himself. Therefore Manoah and his wife conclude, from this evidence, that they have seen, not a mere angel, but God himself. Hence he says, "We shall surely die, because we have seen God." When his wife replies, "If the Lord were pleased to kill us, he would not have received" a sacrifice "at our hands," she clearly acknowledges him to be God, who before is called an angel. Moreover, the reply of the angel himself removes every doubt: "Why askest thou after my name, seeing it is wonderful?" So much the more detestable is the impiety of Servetus, in asserting that God never appeared to Abraham and the other patriarchs, but that they worshipped an angel in his stead. But the orthodox doctors of the church have truly and wisely understood and taught, that the same chief angel was the Word of God, who even then began to perform some services introductory to his execution of the office of Mediator. For though he was not yet incarnate, he descended, as it were, in a mediatorial capacity, that he might approach the faithful with greater familiarity. His familiar intercourse with men gave him the name of an angel; yet he still retained what properly belonged to him, and continued the ineffably glorious God. The same truth is attested by Hosea, who, after relating the wrestling of Jacob with an angel, says, "The Lord (Jehovah) God of hosts; Jehovah is his memorial." Servetus again cavils, that God employed the person of an angel; as though the prophet did not confirm what had been delivered by Moses,—"Wherefore is it that thou dost ask after my name?" And the confession of the holy patriarch, when he says, "I have seen God face to face," sufficiently declares, that he was not a created angel, but one in whom resided the fulness of Deity. Hence, also, the representation of Paul, that Christ was the conductor of the people in the wilderness; because, though the time of his humiliation was not yet arrived, the eternal Word then exhibited a type of the office to which he was appointed. Now, if the second chapter of Zechariah be strictly and coolly examined, the angel who sends another angel is immediately pronounced the God of hosts, and supreme power is ascribed to him. I omit testimonies innumerable on which our faith safely rests, although they have little influence on the Jews. For when it is said in Isaiah, "Lo, this is our God; we have waited for him, and he will save us; this is Jehovah;" all who have eyes may perceive that this is God, who arises for the salvation of his people. And the emphatical repetition of these pointed expressions forbids an application of this passage to any other than to Christ. But still more plain and decisive is a passage of Malachi, where he prophesies, that "the Lord, who was then sought, should come into his temple." The temple was exclusively consecrated to the one Most High God; yet the prophet claims it as belonging to Christ. Whence it follows, that he is the same God that was always worshipped among the Jews.

XI. The New Testament abounds with innumerable testimonies. We must, therefore, endeavour briefly to select a few, rather than to collect them all. Though the Apostles spake of him after he had appeared in flesh as the Mediator, yet all that I shall adduce will be adapted to prove his eternal Deity. In the first place, it is worthy of particular observation, that the apostle represents those things which were predicted concerning the eternal God, as either already exhibited in Christ, or to be accomplished in him at some future period. The prediction of Isaiah, that the Lord of Hosts would be "for a stone of stumbling, and for a rock of offence to both the houses of Israel," Paul asserts to have been fulfilled in Christ. Therefore he declares, that Christ is the Lord of Hosts. There is a similar instance in another place: "We shall all stand," says he, "before the judgment-seat of Christ. For it is written, As I live, saith the Lord, every knee shall bow to me, and every tongue shall confess to God." Since God, in Isaiah, declares this concerning himself, and Christ actually exhibits it in his own person, it follows, that he is that very God, whose glory cannot be transferred to another. The apostle's quotation from the Psalms also, in his Epistle to the Ephesians, is evidently applicable to none but God: "When he ascended up on high, he led captivity captive:" understanding that ascension to have been prefigured by the exertions of the Divine power in the signal victories of David over the heathen nations, he signifies, that the text was more fully accomplished in Christ. Thus John attests that it was the glory of the Son which was revealed in a vision to Isaiah; whereas the prophet himself records that he saw the majesty of God. And those praises which the Apostle, in the Epistle to the Hebrews, ascribes to the Son, beyond all doubt most evidently belong to God: "Thou, Lord, in the beginning, hast laid the foundation of the earth; and the heavens are the works of thine hands," &c. Again, "Let all the angels of God worship him." Nor is it any misapplication of them, when he refers them to Christ; since all that is predicted in those Psalms has been accomplished only by him. For it was He who arose and had mercy upon Zion; it was He who claimed as his own the dominion over all nations and islands. And why should John, after having affirmed, at the commencement of his Gospel, that the Word was always God, have hesitated to attribute to Christ the majesty of God? And why should Paul have been afraid to place Christ on the tribunal of God, after having so publicly preached his Divinity, when he called him "God blessed for ever?" And, to show how consistent he is with himself on this subject, he says, also, that "God was manifest in the flesh." If he is "God blessed for ever," he is the same to whom this apostle, in another place, affirms all glory and honour to be due. And he conceals not, but openly proclaims, that, "being in the form of God," he "thought it not robbery to be equal with God, but made himself of no reputation." And, lest the impious might object, that he is a sort of artificial God, John goes further, and affirms, that "This is the true God, and eternal life;" although we ought to be fully satisfied by his being called God, especially by a witness who expressly avers that there are no more gods than one; I mean Paul, who says, "though there be that are called gods, whether in heaven or in earth; to us there is but one God, of whom are all things." When we hear, from the same mouth, that "God was manifested in the flesh," that "God hath purchased the Church with his own blood,"—why do we imagine a second God, whom he by no means acknowledges? And there is no doubt that all the pious were of the same opinion. Thomas, likewise, by publicly confessing him to be "his Lord and God," declares him to be the same true God whom he had always worshipped.

XII. If we judge of his Divinity from the works which the Scriptures attribute to him, it will thence appear with increasing evidence. For when he said, that he had, from the beginning, continually coöperated with the Father, the Jews, stupid as they were about his other declarations, yet perceived, that he assumed to himself Divine power; and, therefore, as John informs us, they "sought the more to kill him; because he not only had broken the sabbath, but said also that God was his Father, making himself equal with God." How great, then, must be our stupidity, if we perceive not this passage to be a plain assertion of his Divinity! To preside over the world by his almighty providence, and to govern all things by the rod of his own power, (which the Apostle attributes to him,) belongs exclusively to the Creator. And he participates with the Father, not only in the government of the world, but also in all other offices, which cannot be communicated to creatures. The Lord proclaims, by the prophet, "I, even I, am he that blotteth out thy transgressions, for mine own sake." According to this declaration, when the Jews thought that Christ committed an injury against God, by undertaking to forgive sins, he not only asserted in express terms, that this power belonged to him, but proved it by a miracle. We see, therefore, that he hath not the ministry, but the power of remission of sins, which the Lord declares shall never be transferred from himself to another. Is it not the prerogative of God alone to examine and penetrate the secret thoughts of the heart? Yet Christ possessed that power; which is a proof of his Divinity.

XIII. But with what perspicuity of evidence does it appear in his miracles! Though I grant that the Prophets and Apostles performed miracles similar and equal to his, yet there is a considerable difference in this respect, that they, in their ministry, dispensed the favours of God, whereas his miracles were performed by his exertions of his own power. He sometimes, indeed, used prayer, that he might glorify the Father; but, in most instances, we perceive the manifest displays of his own power. And how should not he be the true author of miracles, who, by his own authority, committed the dispensation of them to others? For the Evangelists relate, that he gave his Apostles power to raise the dead, to heal the leprous, to cast out devils, &c. And they performed that ministry in such a manner, as plainly to discover, that the power proceeded solely from Christ. "In the name of Jesus Christ," says Peter, "arise and walk." It is no wonder, therefore, that Christ should bring forward his miracles, to convince the incredulity of the Jews, since, being performed by his own power, they afforded most ample evidence of his Divinity. Besides, if out of God there be no salvation, no righteousness, no life, but Christ contains all these things in himself, it certainly demonstrates him to be God. Let it not be objected, that life and salvation are infused into him by God; for he is not said to have received salvation, but to be himself salvation. And if no one be good but God alone, how can he be a mere man who is, I will not say good and righteous, but goodness and righteousness itself? Even from the beginning of the creation, according to the testimony of an Evangelist, "in him was life; and the life" then existed as "the light of men." Supported by such proofs, therefore, we venture to repose our faith and hope on him; whereas we know that it is impious and sacrilegious for any man to place his confidence in creatures. He says, "Ye believe in God, believe also in me." And in this sense Paul interprets two passages of Isaiah—"Whosoever believeth on him shall not be ashamed." Again, "There shall be a root of Jesse, that shall rise to reign over the Gentiles; in him shall the Gentiles trust." And why should we search for more testimonies from Scripture, when this declaration occurs so frequently, "He that believeth on me hath everlasting life"? The invocation, arising from faith, is also directed to him; which, nevertheless, peculiarly belongs, if any thing peculiarly belongs, to the Divine majesty. For a prophet says, "Whosoever shall call on the name of the Lord (Jehovah) shall be delivered." And Solomon, "The name of the Lord is a strong tower: the righteous runneth into it, and is safe." But the name of Christ is invoked for salvation: it follows, therefore, that he is Jehovah. Moreover, we have an example of such invocation in Stephen, when he says, "Lord Jesus, receive my spirit." And afterwards in the whole Church, as Ananias testifies in the same book: "Lord,

I have heard by many of this man, how much evil he hath done to thy saints—that call on thy name." And to make it more clearly understood, that "all the fulness of the Godhead dwelleth bodily in Christ," the Apostle confesses that he had introduced among the Corinthians no other doctrine than the knowledge of him, and that this had been the only subject of his preaching. What a remarkable and important consideration is it, that the name of the Son only is preached to us, whereas God commands us to glory in the knowledge of himself alone! Who can dare to assert that he is a mere creature, the knowledge of whom is our only glory? It must also be remarked, that the salutations prefixed to the epistles of Paul implore the same blessings from the Son as from the Father; whence we learn, not only that those things, which our heavenly Father bestows, are obtained for us by his intercession, but that the Son, by a communion of power, is himself the author of them. This practical knowledge is unquestionably more certain and solid than any idle speculation. For then the pious mind has the nearest view of the Divine presence, and almost touches it, when it experiences itself to be quickened, illuminated, saved, justified, and sanctified.

XIV. Wherefore the proof of the Deity of the Spirit must be derived principally from the same sources. There is no obscurity in the testimony of Moses, in the history of the creation, that the Spirit of God was expanded on the abyss or chaos; for it signifies, not only that the beautiful state of the world which we now behold owes its preservation to the power of the Spirit, but that, previously to its being thus adorned, the Spirit was engaged in brooding over the confused mass. The declaration of Isaiah bids defiance to all cavils: "And now the Lord God, and his Spirit, hath sent me." For the Holy Spirit is united in the exercise of supreme power in the mission of Prophets, which is a proof of his Divine majesty. But the best confirmation, as I have remarked, we shall derive from familiar experience. For what the Scriptures ascribe to him, and what we ourselves learn by the certain experience of piety, is not at all applicable to any creature. For it is he who, being universally diffused, sustains and animates all things in heaven and in earth. And this very thing excludes him from the number of creatures, that he is circumscribed by no limits, but transfuses through all his own vigorous influence, to inspire them with being, life, and motion: this is clearly a work of Deity. Again, if regeneration to an incorruptible life be more important and excellent than any present life, what must we think of him from whose power it proceeds? But the Scripture teaches, in various places, that he is the author of regeneration by a power not derived, but properly his own; and not of regeneration only, but likewise of the future immortality. Finally, to him, as well as to the Son, are applied all those offices which are peculiar to Deity. For he "searcheth even the deep things of God," who admits no creature to a share in his councils. He bestows wisdom and the faculty of speech; whereas the Lord declares to Moses, that this can only be done by himself. So through him we attain to a participation of God, to feel his vivifying energy upon us. Our justification is his work. From him proceed power, sanctification, truth, grace, and every other blessing we can conceive; since there is but one Spirit, from whom every kind of gifts descends. For this passage of Paul is worthy of particular attention: "There are diversities of gifts, and there are differences of administrations, but the same Spirit;" because it represents him, not only as the principle and source of them, but also as the author; which is yet more clearly expressed a little after in these words: "All these worketh that only and the self-same Spirit, dividing to every man severally as he will." For if he were not a subsistence in the Deity, judgment and voluntary determination would never be ascribed to him. Paul, therefore, very clearly attributes to the Spirit Divine power, and thereby demonstrates him to be an hypostasis or subsistence in God.

XV. Nor does the Scripture, when it speaks of him, refrain from giving him the appellation of God. For Paul concludes that we are the temple of God, because his Spirit dwelleth in us. This must not be passed over without particular notice; for the frequent promises of God, that he will choose us for a temple for himself, receive no other accomplishment, than by the inhabitation of his Spirit in us. Certainly, as Augustine excellently observes, "If we were commanded to erect to the Spirit a temple of wood and stone, forasmuch as God is the sole object of worship, it would be a clear proof of his Divinity; how much clearer, then, is the proof, now that we are commanded, not to erect one, but to be ourselves his temples!" And the Apostle calls us sometimes the temple of God, and sometimes the temple of the Holy Spirit, both in the same signification. Peter, reprehending Ananias for having "lied to the Holy Ghost," told him that he had "not lied unto men, but unto God." And where Isaiah introduces the Lord of hosts as the speaker, Paul informs us that it is the Holy Spirit who speaks. Indeed, while the Prophets invariably declare, that the words which they utter are those of the Lord of hosts, Christ and the Apostles refer them to the Holy Spirit; whence it follows, that he is the true Jehovah, who is the primary author of the prophecies. Again, God complains that his anger was provoked by the perverseness of the people; Isaiah, in reference to the same conduct, says, that "they vexed his Holy Spirit." Lastly, if blasphemy against the Spirit be not forgiven, either in this world or in that which is to come, whilst a man may obtain pardon who has been guilty of blasphemy against the Son, this is an open declaration of his Divine majesty, to defame or degrade which is an inexpiable crime. I intentionally pass over many testimonies which were used by the fathers. To them there appeared much plausibility in citing this passage from David, "By the word of the Lord were the heavens made, and all the host of them by the breath of his mouth;" to prove that the creation of the world was the work of the Holy Spirit, as well as of the Son. But since a repetition of the same thing twice is common in the Psalms, and in Isaiah "the spirit of his mouth" means the same as "his word," this is but a weak argument. Therefore I have determined to confine myself to a sober statement of those evidences on which pious minds may satisfactorily rest.

XVI. As God afforded a clearer manifestation of himself at the advent of Christ, the three Persons also then became better known. Among many testimonies, let us be satisfied with this one: Paul connects together these three, Lord, Faith, and Baptism, in such a manner as to reason from one to another. Since there is but one faith, hence he proves that there is but one Lord; since there is but one baptism, he shows that there is also but one faith. Therefore, if we are initiated by baptism into the faith and religion of one God, we must necessarily suppose him to be the true God, into whose name we are baptized. Nor can it be doubted but that in this solemn commission, "Baptize them in the name of the Father, and of the Son, and of the Holy Ghost," Christ intended to testify, that the perfect light of faith was now exhibited. For this is equivalent to being baptized into the name of the one God, who hath clearly manifested himself in the Father, Son, and Spirit; whence it evidently appears, that in the Divine Essence there exist three Persons, in whom is known the one God. And truly, since faith ought not to be looking about hither and thither, or to be wandering through the varieties of inconstancy, but to direct its views towards the one God, to be fixed on him, and to adhere to him,—it may easily be proved from these premises, that, if there be various kinds of faith, there must also be a plurality of gods. Baptism, being a sacrament of faith, confirms to us the unity of God, because it is but one. Hence, also, we conclude, that it is not lawful to be baptized, except into the name of the one God; because we embrace the faith of him, into whose name we are baptized. What, then, was intended by Christ, when he commanded baptism to be administered in the name of the Father, and of the Son, and of the Holy Spirit, but that one faith ought to be exercised in the Father, Son, and Spirit? and what is that but a clear testimony, that the Father, the Son, and the Holy Spirit, are the one God? Therefore, since it is an undeniable truth, that there is one God, and only one, we conclude the Word and Spirit to be no other than the very Essence of the Deity. The greatest degree of folly was betrayed by the Arians, who confessed the Divinity of the Son, but denied him to possess the substance of God. Nor were the Macedonians free from a similar delusion, who would explain the term "Spirit" to mean only the gifts of grace conferred upon man. For as wisdom, understanding, prudence, fortitude, and the fear of the Lord, proceed from him, so he alone is the Spirit of wisdom, prudence, fortitude, and piety. Nor is he himself divided according to the distribution of his graces; but, as the Apostle declares, how variously soever they are divided, he always remains one and the same.

XVII. On the other hand, also, we find in the Scriptures a distinction between the Father and the Word, between the Word and the Spirit; in the discussion of which the magnitude of the mystery reminds us that we ought to proceed with the utmost reverence and sobriety. I am exceedingly pleased with this observation of Gregory Nazianzen: "I cannot think of the *one*, but I am immediately surrounded with the splendour of the *three*; nor can I clearly discover the *three*, but I am suddenly carried back to the *one*." Wherefore let us not imagine such a trinity of Persons, as includes an idea of separation, or does not immediately recall us to the unity. The names of Father, Son, and Spirit, certainly imply a real distinction; let no one suppose them to be mere epithets, by which God is variously designated from his works; but it is a distinction, not a division. The passages already cited show, that the Son has a property, by which he is distinguished from the Father; because the Word had not been with God, or had his glory with the Father, unless he had been distinct from him. He likewise distinguishes the Father from himself, when he says, "that there is another that beareth witness of him." And to the same effect is what is declared in another place, that the Father created all things by the Word; which he could not have done, unless he had been in some sense distinct from him. Besides, the Father descended not to the earth, but he who came forth from the Father. The Father neither died nor rose again, but he who was sent by the Father. Nor did this distinction commence at the incarnation, but it is evident, that, before that period, he was the only begotten in the bosom of the Father. For who can undertake to assert, that the Son first entered into the bosom of the Father, when he descended from heaven to assume a human nature? He, therefore, was in the bosom of the Father before, and possessed his glory with the Father. The distinction between the Holy Spirit and the Father is announced by Christ, when he says, that he "proceedeth from the Father." But how often does he represent him as another, distinct from himself! as when he promises that "another Comforter" should be sent, and in many other places.

XVIII. I doubt the propriety of borrowing similitudes from human things, to express the force of this distinction. The fathers sometimes practise this method; but they likewise confess the great disproportion of all the similitudes which they introduce. Wherefore I greatly dread, in this instance, every degree of presumption; lest the introduction of any thing unseasonable should afford an occasion of calumny to the malicious, or of error to the ignorant. Yet it is not right to be silent on the distinction which we find expressed in the Scriptures; which is this—that to the Father is attributed the principle of action, the fountain and source of all things; to the Son, wisdom, counsel, and the arrangement of all operations; and the power and efficacy of the action is assigned to the Spirit. Moreover, though eternity belongs to the Father, and to the Son and Spirit also, since God can never have been destitute of his wisdom or his power, and in eternity we must not inquire after any thing prior or posterior,—yet the observation of order is not vain or superfluous, while the Father is mentioned as first; in the next place the Son, as from him; and then the Spirit, as from both. For the mind of every man naturally inclines to the consideration, first, of God; secondly, of the wisdom emanating from him; and lastly, of the power by which he executes the decrees of his wisdom. For this reason the Son is said to be from the Father, and the Spirit from both the Father and the Son; and that in various places, but nowhere more clearly than in the eighth chapter of the Epistle to the Romans, where the same Spirit is indifferently denominated "the Spirit of Christ," and "the Spirit of him that raised up Christ from the dead," and that without any impropriety. For Peter also testifies that it was the Spirit of Christ by whom the prophets prophesied; whereas the Scripture so frequently declares that it was the Spirit of God the Father.

XIX. This distinction is so far from opposing the most absolute simplicity and unity of the Divine Being, that it affords a proof that the Son is one God with the Father, because he has the same Spirit with him; and that the Spirit is not a different substance from the Father and the Son, because he is the Spirit of the Father and of the Son. For the whole nature is in each hypostasis, and each has something peculiar to himself. The Father is entirely in the Son, and the Son entirely in the Father, according to his own declaration, "I am in the Father, and the Father in me;" nor do ecclesiastical writers allow that one is divided from the other by any difference of essence. "These distinctive appellations," says Augustine, "denote their reciprocal relations to each other, and not the substance itself, which is but one." This explanation may serve to reconcile the opinions of the fathers, which would otherwise appear totally repugnant to each other. For sometimes they state that the Son originates from the Father, and at other times assert that he has essential Divinity from himself, and so is, together with the Father, the one first cause of all. Augustine, in another place, admirably and perspicuously explains the cause of this diversity, in the following manner: "Christ, considered in himself, is called God; but with relation to the Father, he is called the Son." And again, "The Father, considered in himself, is called God; but with relation to the Son, he is called the Father. He who, with relation to the Son, is called the Father, is not the Son; he who, with relation to the Father, is called the Son, is not the Father; they who are severally called the Father and the Son, are the same God." Therefore, when we speak simply of the Son, without reference to the Father, we truly and properly assert him to be self-existent, and therefore call him the sole first cause; but, when we distinctly treat of the relation between him and the Father, we justly represent him as originating from the Father. The first book of Augustine on the Trinity is entirely occupied with the explication of this subject; and it is far more safe to rest satisfied with that relation which he states, than by curiously penetrating into the sublime mystery, to wander through a multitude of vain speculations.

XX. Therefore, let such as love sobriety, and will be contented with the measure of faith, briefly attend to what is useful to be known; which is, that, when we profess to believe in one God, the word *God* denotes a single and simple essence, in which we comprehend three Persons, or hypostases; and that, therefore, whenever the word *God* is used indefinitely, the Son and Spirit are intended as much as the Father; but when the Son is associated with the Father, that introduces the reciprocal relation of one to the other; and thus we distinguish between the Persons. But, since the peculiar properties of the Persons produce a certain order, so that the original cause is in the Father, whenever the Father and the Son or Spirit are mentioned together, the name of God is peculiarly ascribed to the Father: by this method the unity of the essence is preserved, and the order is retained; which, however, derogates nothing from the Deity of the Son and Spirit. And indeed, as we have already seen that the Apostles assert him to be the Son of God, whom Moses and the Prophets have represented as Jehovah, it is always necessary to recur to the unity of the essence. Wherefore it would be a detestable sacrilege for us to call the Son another God different from the Father; because the simple name of God admits of no relation; nor can God, with respect to himself, be denominated either the one or the other. Now, that the name "Jehovah," in an indefinite sense, is applicable to Christ, appears even from the words of Paul: "for this thing I besought the Lord thrice;" because, after relating the answer of Christ, "My grace is sufficient for thee," he immediately subjoins, "That the power of Christ may rest upon me." For it is certain that the word "Lord" is there used for "Jehovah;" and to restrict it to the person of the Mediator, would be frivolous and puerile, since it is an absolute declaration, containing no comparison between the Son and the Father. And we know that the Apostles, following the custom of the Greek translators, invariably use the word Κυριος, (Lord,) instead of Jehovah. And, not to seek far for an example of this, Paul prayed to the Lord in no other sense than is intended in a passage of Joel, cited by Peter: "Whosoever shall call on the name of the Lord shall be saved." But for the peculiar ascription of this name to the Son, another reason will be given in its proper place; suffice it at present to observe that, when Paul had prayed to God absolutely, he immediately subjoins the name of Christ. Thus also the whole Deity is by Christ himself denominated "a Spirit." For nothing opposes the spirituality of the whole Divine essence, in which are comprehended the Father, the Son, and the Spirit; which is plain from the Scripture. For as we there find God denominated a Spirit, so we find also the Holy Spirit, forasmuch as he is an hypostasis of the whole essence, represented both as the Spirit of God, and as proceeding from God.

XXI. But since Satan, in order to subvert the very foundations of our faith, has always been exciting great contentions concerning the Divine essence of the Son and Spirit, and the distinction of the Persons; and in almost all ages has instigated impious spirits to vex the orthodox teachers on this account; and is also endeavouring, in the present day, with the old embers, to kindle a new flame; it becomes necessary here to refute the perverse and fanciful notions which some persons have imbibed. Hitherto it has been our principal design to instruct the docile, and not to combat the obstinate and contentious: but now, having calmly explained and proved the truth, we must vindicate it from all the cavils of the wicked; although I shall make it my principal study, that those who readily and implicitly attend to the Divine word, may have stable ground on which they may confidently rest. On this, indeed, if on any of the secret mysteries of the Scripture, we ought to philosophize with great sobriety and moderation; and also with extreme caution, lest either our ideas or our language should proceed beyond the limits of the Divine word. For how can the infinite essence of God be defined by the narrow capacity of the human mind, which could never yet certainly determine the nature of the body of the sun, though the object of our daily contemplation? How can the human mind, by its own efforts, penetrate into an examination of the essence of God, when it is totally ignorant of its own? Wherefore let us freely leave to God the knowledge of himself. For "he alone," as Hilary says, "is a competent witness for himself, being only known by himself." And we shall certainly leave it to him, if our conceptions of him correspond to the manifestations which he has given us of himself, and our inquiries concerning him are confined to his word. There are extant on this argument five homilies of Chrysostom against the Anomœi; which, however, were not sufficient to restrain the presumptuous garrulity of those sophists. For they discovered no greater modesty in this instance than in every other. The very unhappy consequences of this temerity should warn us to study this question with more docility than subtlety, and not allow ourselves to investigate God any where but in his sacred word, or to form any ideas of him but such as are agreeable to his word, or to speak any thing concerning him but what is derived from the same word. But if the distinction of Father, Son, and Spirit, in the one Deity, as it is not easy to be comprehended, occasions some understandings more labour and trouble than is desirable, let them remember that the mind of man, when it indulges its curiosity, enters into a labyrinth; and let them submit to be guided by the heavenly oracles, however they may not comprehend the height of this mystery.

XXII. To compose a catalogue of the errors, by which the purity of the faith has been attacked on this point of doctrine, would be too prolix and tedious, without being profitable; and most of the heretics so strenuously exerted themselves to effect the total extinction of the Divine glory by their gross reveries, that they thought it sufficient to unsettle and disturb the inexperienced. From a few men there soon arose numerous sects, of whom some would divide the Divine essence, and others would confound the distinction which subsists between the Persons. But if we maintain, what has already been sufficiently demonstrated from the Scripture, that the essence of the one God, which pertains to the Father, to the Son, and to the Spirit, is simple and undivided, and, on the other hand, that the Father is, by some property, distinguished from the Son, and likewise the Son from the Spirit, the gate will be shut, not only against Arius and Sabellius, but also against all the other ancient heresiarchs. But since our own times have witnessed some madmen, as Servetus and his followers, who have involved every thing in new subtleties, a brief exposure of their fallacies will not be unuseful. The word *Trinity* was so odious and even detestable to Servetus, that he asserted all Trinitarians, as he called them, to be Atheists. I omit his impertinent and scurrilous language, but this was the substance of his speculations: That it is representing God as consisting of three parts, when three Persons are said to subsist in his essence, and that this triad is merely imaginary, being repugnant to the Divine unity. At the same time, he maintained the Persons to be certain external ideas, which have no real subsistence in the Divine essence, but give us a figurative representation of God, under this or the other form; and that in the beginning there was no distinction in God, because the Word was once the same as the Spirit; but that, after Christ appeared God of God, there emanated from him another God, even the Spirit. Though he sometimes glosses over his impertinencies with allegories, as when he says, that the eternal Word of God was the Spirit of Christ with God, and the reflection of his image, and that the Spirit was a shadow of the Deity, yet he afterwards destroys the Deity of both, asserting that, according to the mode of dispensation, there is a part of God in both the Son and the Spirit; just as the same Spirit, substantially diffused in us, and even in wood and stones, is a portion of the Deity. What he broached concerning the Person of the Mediator, we shall examine in the proper place. But this monstrous fiction, that a Divine Person is nothing but a visible appearance of the glory of God, will not need a prolix refutation. For when John pronounces that the Word (Λογος) was God before the creation of the world, he sufficiently discriminates him from an ideal form. But if then also, and from the remotest eternity, that Word (Λογος) who was God, was with the Father, and possessed his own glory with the Father, he certainly could not be an external or figurative splendour; but it necessarily follows, that he was a real hypostasis, subsisting in God himself. But although no mention is made of the Spirit, but in the history of the creation of the world, yet he is there introduced, not as a shadow, but as the essential power of God, since Moses relates that the chaotic mass was supported by him. It then appeared, therefore, that the eternal Spirit had always existed in the Deity, since he cherished and sustained the confused matter of the heaven and earth, till it attained a state of beauty and order. He certainly could not then be an image or representation of God, according to the dreams of Servetus. But in other places he is constrained to make a fuller disclosure of his impiety, saying that God, in his eternal reason, decreeing for himself a visible Son, has visibly exhibited himself in this manner; for if this be true, there is no other Divinity left to Christ, than as he has been appointed a Son by an eternal decree of God. Besides, he so transforms those phantasms, which he substitutes instead of the hypostases, that he hesitates not to imagine new accidents or properties in God. But the most execrable blasphemy of all is, his promiscuous confusion of the Son of God and the Spirit with all the creatures. For he asserts that in the Divine essence there are parts and divisions, every portion of which is God; and especially that the souls of the faithful are coëternal and consubstantial with God; though in another place he assigns substantial Deity, not only to the human soul, but to all created things.

XXIII. From the same corrupt source has proceeded another heresy, equally monstrous. For some worthless men, to escape the odium and disgrace which attended the impious tenets of Servetus, have confessed, indeed, that there are three Persons, but with this explanation, that the Father, who alone is truly and properly God, hath created the Son and Spirit, and transfused his Deity into them. Nor do they refrain from this dreadful manner of expressing themselves, that the Father is distinguished from the Son and Spirit, as being the sole possessor of the Divine essence. Their first plea in support of this notion is, that Christ is commonly called the Son of God; whence they conclude that no other is properly God but the Father. But they observe not, that although the name of God is common also to the Son, yet that it is sometimes ascribed to the Father (κατ' ἐξοχην) by way of eminence, because he is the fountain and original of the Deity; and this in order to denote the simple unity of the essence. They object, that if he is truly the Son of God, it is absurd to account him the Son of a Person. I reply, that both are true; that he is the Son of God, because he is the Word begotten of the Father before time began, for we are not yet speaking of the Person of the Mediator; and to be explicit, we must notice the Person, that the name of God may not be understood absolutely, but for the Father; for if we acknowledge no other to be God than the Father, it will be a manifest degradation of the dignity of the Son. Whenever mention is made of the Deity, therefore, there must no opposition be admitted between the Father and the Son, as though the name of the true God belonged exclusively to the Father. For surely the God who appeared to Isaiah, was the only true God; whom, nevertheless, John affirms to have been Christ. He likewise, who by the mouth of Isaiah declared that he was to be a rock of offence to the Jews, was the only true God; whom Paul pronounces to have been Christ. He who proclaims by Isaiah, "As I live, every knee shall bow to me," is the only true God; but Paul applies the same to Christ. To the same purpose are the testimonies recited by the Apostle—"Thou, Lord, hast laid the foundation of the earth and the heavens;" and "Let all the angels of God worship him." These ascriptions belong only to the one true God; whereas he contends that they are properly applied to Christ. Nor is there any force in that cavil, that what is proper to God is transferred to Christ, because he is the brightness of his glory. For, since the name Jehovah is used in each of these passages, it follows that in respect of his Deity he is self-existent. For, if he is Jehovah, he cannot be denied to be the same God, who in another place proclaims by Isaiah, "I am the first and I am the last; and beside me there is no God." That passage in Jeremiah also deserves our attention—"The gods that have not made the heavens and the earth, even they shall perish from the earth, and from under these heavens;" whilst, on the contrary, it must be acknowledged, that the Deity of the Son of God is frequently proved by Isaiah from the creation of the world. But how shall the Creator, who gives existence to all, not be self-existent, but derive his essence from another? For whoever asserts that the Son owes his essence to the Father, denies him to be self-existent. But this is contradicted by the Holy Spirit, who gives him the name of Jehovah. Now, if we admit the whole essence to be solely in the Father, either it will be divisible, or it will be taken away from the Son; and so, being despoiled of his essence, he will be only a titular god. The Divine essence, according to these triflers, belongs solely to the Father, inasmuch as he alone possesses it, and is the author of the essence of the Son. Thus the Divinity of the Son will be a kind of emanation from the essence of God, or a derivation of a part from the whole. Now, they must of necessity concede, from their own premises, that the Spirit is the Spirit of the Father only; because if he be a derivation from the original essence, which belongs exclusively to the Father, he cannot be accounted the Spirit of the Son; which is refuted by the testimony of Paul, where he makes him common to Christ and the Father. Besides, if the Person of the Father be expunged from the Trinity, wherein will he differ from the Son and Spirit, but in being himself the sole Deity? They confess that Christ is God, and yet differs from the Father. Some distinctive character is necessary, also, to discriminate the Father from the Son. They who place this in the essence, manifestly destroy the true Deity of Christ, which cannot exist independently of the essence, that is, of the entire essence. The Father certainly cannot differ from the Son, unless he have something peculiar to himself, which is not common to the Son. What will they find, by which to distinguish him? If the difference be in the essence, let them tell us whether he has communicated the same to the Son. But this could not be done partially; for it would be an abomination to fabricate a demigod. Besides, this would miserably dismember the Divine essence. The necessary conclusion then is, that it is entirely and perfectly common to the Father and the Son. And if this be true, there cannot, in respect of the essence, be any difference between them. If it be objected that the Father, notwithstanding this communication of his essence, remains the only God with whom the essence continues, then Christ must be a figurative god, a god in appearance and name only, not in reality; because nothing is more proper to God than to be, according to that declaration, "I AM hath sent me unto you."

XXIV. We might readily prove from many passages the falsehood of their assumption, that, whenever the name of God is mentioned absolutely in the Scripture, it means only the Father. And in those places which they cite in their own defence, they shamefully betray their ignorance, since the Son is there added; from which it appears, that the name of God is used in a relative sense, and therefore is particularly restricted to the Person of the Father. Their objection, that, unless the Father alone were the true God, he would himself be his own Father, is answered in a word. For there is no absurdity in the name of God, for the sake of dignity and order, being peculiarly given to him, who not only hath begotten of himself his own wisdom, but is also the God of the Mediator, of which I shall treat more at large in its proper place. For since Christ was manifested in the flesh, he is called the Son of God, not only as he was the eternal Word begotten of the Father before time began, but because he assumed the person and office of a Mediator, to unite us to God. And since they so presumptuously exclude the Son from Divine honours, I would wish to be informed, when he declares that there is none good but the one God, whether he deprives himself of all goodness. I speak not of his human nature, lest they should object, that, whatever goodness it had, it was gratuitously conferred on it. I demand whether the eternal Word of God be good or not. If they answer in the negative, they are sufficiently convicted of impiety; and if in the affirmative, they cut the throat of their own system. But though, at the first glance, Christ seems to deny himself the appellation of good, he furnishes, notwithstanding, a further confirmation of our opinion. For, as that is a title which peculiarly belongs to the one God, forasmuch as he had been saluted as good, merely according to a common custom, by his rejection of false honour, he suggested that the goodness which he possessed was Divine. I demand, also, when Paul affirms that God alone is immortal, wise, and true, whether he thereby degrades Christ to the rank of those who are mortal, unwise, and false. Shall not he then be immortal who from the beginning was life itself, and the giver of immortality to angels? Shall not he be wise who is the eternal Wisdom of God? Shall not he be true who is truth itself? I demand further, whether they think that Christ ought to be worshipped. For, if he justly claims this as his right, that every knee should bow before him, it follows that he is that God, who, in the law, prohibited the worship of any one but himself. If they will have this passage in Isaiah, "I am, and there is no God besides me," to be understood solely of the Father, I retort this testimony on themselves; since we see that whatever belongs to God is attributed to Christ. Nor is there any room for their cavil, that Christ was exalted in the humanity in which he had been abased; and that, with regard to his humanity, all power was given to him in heaven and in earth; because, although the regal and judicial majesty extends to the whole Person of the Mediator, yet, had he not been God manifested in the flesh, he could not have been exalted to such an eminence, without God being in opposition to himself. And Paul excellently determines this controversy, by informing us that he was equal with God, before he abased himself under the form of a servant. Now, how could this equality subsist, unless he had been that God whose name is Jah and Jehovah, who rides on the cherubim, whose kingdom is universal and everlasting? No clamour of theirs can deprive Christ of another declaration of Isaiah: "Lo, this is our God, we have waited for him;" since in these words he describes the advent of God the Redeemer, not only for the deliverance of the people from exile in Babylon, but also for the complete restoration of the church. Nor do they gain any thing by another cavil, that Christ was God in his Father. For although we confess, in point of order and degree, that the Father is the fountain of the Deity, yet we pronounce it a detestable figment, that the essence belongs exclusively to the Father, as though he were the author of the Deity of the Son; because, on this supposition, either the essence would be divided, or Christ would be only a titular and imaginary god. If they admit that the Son is God, but inferior to the Father, then in him the essence must be begotten and created, which in the Father is unbegotten and uncreated. I know that some scorners ridicule our concluding a distinction of Persons from the words of Moses, where he introduces God thus speaking: "Let us make man in our image." Yet pious readers perceive how frigidly and foolishly Moses would have introduced this conference, if in one God there had not subsisted a plurality of Persons. Now, it is certain that they whom the Father addressed, were uncreated; but there is nothing uncreated, except the one God himself. Now, therefore, unless they grant that the power to create, and the authority to command, were common to the Father, the Son, and the Spirit, it will follow, that God did not speak thus within himself, but directed his conversation to some exterior agents. Lastly, one place will easily remove their two objections at once. For when Christ himself declares, that God is a Spirit, it would be unreasonable to restrict this solely to the Father, as though the Word were not also of a spiritual nature. But if the name of Spirit is equally as applicable to the Son as to the Father, I conclude that the Son is comprehended under the indefinite name of God. Yet he immediately subjoins, that none are approved worshippers of the Father, but those who worship him in spirit and in truth. Whence follows another consequence, that, because Christ performs the office of a Teacher, in a station of inferiority, he ascribes the name of God to the Father, not to destroy his own Deity, but by degrees to raise us to the knowledge of it.

XXV. But they deceive themselves in dreaming of three separate individuals, each of them possessing a part of the Divine essence. We teach, according to the Scriptures, that there is essentially but one God; and, therefore, that the essence of both the Son and the Spirit is unbegotten. But since the Father is first in order, and hath of himself begotten his wisdom, therefore, as has before been observed, he is justly esteemed the original and fountain of the whole Divinity. Thus God, indefinitely, is unbegotten; and the Father also is unbegotten with regard to his Person. They even foolishly suppose, that our opinion implies a quaternity; whereas they are guilty of falsehood and calumny, in ascribing to us a figment of their own; as though we pretended that the three Persons are as so many streams proceeding from one essence, when it is evident, from our writings, that we separate not the Persons from the essence, but, though they subsist in it, make a distinction between them. If the persons were separated from the essence, there would perhaps be some probability in their argument; but then there would be a trinity of Gods, not a trinity of persons contained in one God. This solves their frivolous question, whether the essence concurs to the formation of the Trinity; as though we imagined three Gods to descend from it. Their objection, that then the Trinity would be without God, is equally impertinent. Because, though it concurs not to the distinction as a part or member, yet the Persons are not independent of it, nor separate from it; for the Father, unless he were God, could not be the Father; and the Son is the Son only as he is God. Therefore we say, that the Deity is absolutely self-existent; whence we confess, also, that the Son, as God, independently of the consideration of Person, is self-existent; but as the Son, we say, that he is of the Father. Thus his essence is unoriginated; but the origin of his Person is God himself. And, indeed, the orthodox writers, who have written on the Trinity, have referred this name only to the Persons; since to comprehend the essence in that distinction, were not only an absurd error, but a most gross impiety. For it is evident that those who maintain that the Trinity consists in a union of the Essence, the Son, and the Spirit, annihilate the essence of the Son and of the Spirit; otherwise the parts would be destroyed by being confounded together; which is a fault in every distinction. Finally, if the words *Father* and *God* were synonymous—if the Father were the author of the Deity—nothing would be left in the Son but a mere shadow; nor would the Trinity be any other than a conjunction of the one God with two created things.

XXVI. Their objection, that Christ, if he be properly God, is not rightly called the Son of God, has already been answered; for when a comparison is made between one Person and another, the word *God* is not used indefinitely, but is restricted to the Father, as being the fountain of the Deity, not with regard to the essence, as fanatics falsely pretend, but in respect of order. This is the sense in which we ought to understand that declaration of Christ to his Father: "This is life eternal, that they might know thee, the only true God, and Jesus Christ, whom thou hast sent." For, speaking in the capacity of Mediator, he holds an intermediate station between God and men; yet without any diminution of his majesty. For, although he abased himself, yet he lost not his glory with the Father, which was hidden from the world. Thus the Apostle to the Hebrews, though he acknowledges that Christ was made for a short time inferior to the angels, yet, nevertheless, hesitates not to assert, that he is the eternal God, who laid the foundation of the earth. We must remember, therefore, that whenever Christ, in the capacity of Mediator, addresses the Father, he comprehends, under the name of God, the Divinity which belongs also to himself. Thus, when he said to his Apostles, "I go unto the Father, for my Father is greater than I," he attributes not to himself a secondary Divinity, as if he were inferior to the Father with respect to the eternal essence, but because, having obtained the glory of heaven, he gathers together the faithful to a participation of it with him; he represents the Father to be in a station superior to himself, just as the illustrious perfection of the splendour which appears in heaven excels that degree of glory which was visible in him during his incarnate state. For the same reason, Paul says, in another place, that Christ "shall deliver up the kingdom to God, even the Father, that God may be all in all." Nothing would be more absurd than to deny perpetual duration to the Deity of Christ. Now, if he will never cease to be the Son of God, but will remain for ever the same as he has been from the beginning, it follows, that by the name *Father* is intended the one sole Divine essence, which is common to them both. And it is certain that Christ descended to us, in order that, exalting us to the Father, he might at the same time exalt us to himself also, as being one with the Father. It is therefore neither lawful nor right to restrict the name of God exclusively to the Father, and to deny it to the Son. For even on this very account John asserts him to be the true God, that no one might suppose, that he possessed only a secondary degree of Deity, inferior to the Father. And I wonder what can be the meaning of these fabricators of new gods, when, after confessing that Christ is the true

God, they immediately exclude him from the Deity of the Father; as though there could be any true God but one alone, or as though a transfused Divinity were any thing but a novel fiction.

XXVII. Their accumulation of numerous passages from Irenæus, where he asserts the Father of Christ to be the only and eternal God of Israel, is a proof either of shameful ignorance, or of consummate wickedness. For they ought to have considered, that that holy man was then engaged in a controversy with some madmen, who denied that the Father of Christ was the same God that has spoken by Moses and the Prophets, but maintained that he was I know not what sort of phantasm, produced from the corruption of the world. His only object, therefore, is to show that no other God is revealed in the Scripture than the Father of Christ, and that it is impious to imagine any other; and therefore we need not wonder at his frequently concluding, that there never was any other God of Israel than he who was preached by Christ and his Apostles. So, now, on the other hand, when a different error is to be opposed, we shall truly assert, that the God who appeared formerly to the patriarchs, was no other than Christ. If it be objected that it was the Father, we are prepared to reply, that, while we contend for the Divinity of the Son, we by no means reject that of the Father. If the reader attends to this design of Irenæus, all contention will cease. Moreover, the whole controversy is easily decided by the sixth chapter of the third book, where the good man insists on this one point: That he who is absolutely and indefinitely called God in the Scripture, is the only true God; but that the name of God is given absolutely to Christ. Let us remember that the point at issue, as appears from the whole treatise, and particularly from the forty-sixth chapter of the second book, was this: That the appellation of Father is not given in an enigmatical and parabolical sense to one who is not truly God. Besides, in another place he contends, that the Son is called God, as well as the Father, by the Prophets and Apostles. He afterwards states how Christ, who is Lord, and King, and God, and Judge of all, received power from him who is God of all; and that is with relation to the subjection in which he was humbled even to the death of the cross. And a little after he affirms, that the Son is the Creator of heaven and earth, who gave the law by the hand of Moses, and appeared to the patriarchs. Now, if any one pretends that Irenæus acknowledges the Father alone as the God of Israel, I shall reply, as is clearly maintained by the same writer, that Christ is one and the same; as also he applies to him the prophecy of Habakkuk: "God shall come from the south." To the same purpose is what we find in the ninth chapter of the fourth book: "Therefore Christ himself is, with the Father, the God of the living." And in the twelfth chapter of the same book he states, that Abraham believed in God, inasmuch as Christ is the Creator of heaven and earth, and the only God.

XXVIII. Their pretensions to the sanction of Tertullian are equally unfounded, for, notwithstanding the occasional harshness and obscurity of his mode of expression, yet he unequivocally teaches the substance of the doctrine which we are defending; that is, that whereas there is one God, yet by dispensation or economy there is his Word; that there is but one God in the unity of the substance, but that the unity, by a mysterious dispensation, is disposed into a trinity; that there are three, not in condition, but in degree; not in substance, but in form; not in power, but in order. He says, indeed, that he maintains the Son to be second to the Father; but he applies this only to the distinction of the Persons. He says somewhere, that the Son is visible; but after having stated arguments on both sides, he concludes that, as the Word, he is invisible. Lastly, his assertion that the Father is designated by his Person, proves him to be at the greatest distance from the notion which we are refuting. And though he acknowledges no other God than the Father, yet the explanations which he gives in the immediate context show that he speaks not to the exclusion of the Son, when he denies the existence of any other God than the Father; and that therefore the unity of Divine government is not violated by the distinction of persons. And from the nature and design of his argument it is easy to gather the meaning of his words. For he contends, in opposition to Praxeas, that although God is distinguished into three Persons, yet neither is there a plurality of gods, nor is the unity divided. And because, according to the erroneous notion of Praxeas, Christ could not be God, without being the Father, therefore Tertullian bestows so much labour upon the distinction. His calling the Word and Spirit a portion of the whole, though a harsh expression, yet is excusable; since it has no reference to the substance, but only denotes the disposition and economy, which belongs solely to the Persons, according to the testimony of Tertullian himself. Hence also that question, "How many Persons suppose you that there are, O most perverse Praxeas, but as many as there are names?" So, a little after, "that they may believe the Father and the Son, both in their names and Persons." These arguments, I conceive, will suffice to refute the impudence of those who make use of the authority of Tertullian in order to deceive the minds of the simple.

XXIX. And certainly, whoever will diligently compare the writings of the fathers, will find in Irenæus nothing different from what was advanced by others who succeeded him. Justin Martyr is one of the most ancient; and he agrees with us in every point. They may object that the Father of Christ is denominated the one God by him as well as by the rest. The same is asserted also by Hilary, and even in harsher terms: he says, that eternity is in the Father; but does this imply a denial of the Divine essence to the Son? On the contrary, he had no other design than to maintain the same faith which we hold. Nevertheless, they are not ashamed to cull out mutilated passages, in order to induce a belief that he patronized their error. If they wish any authority to be attached to their quotation of Ignatius, let them prove that the Apostles delivered any law concerning Lent, and similar corruptions; for nothing can be more absurd than the impertinencies which have been published under the name of Ignatius. Wherefore their impudence is more intolerable, who disguise themselves under such false colours for the purpose of deception. Moreover, the consent of antiquity manifestly appears from this circumstance, that in the Nicene Council, Arius never dared to defend himself by the authority of any approved writer; and not one of the Greek or Latin fathers, who were there united against him, excused himself as at all dissenting from his predecessors. With regard to Augustine, who experienced great hostility from these disturbers, his diligent examination of all the writings of the earlier fathers, and his respectful attention to them, need not be mentioned. If he differs from them in the smallest particulars, he assigns the reasons which oblige him to dissent from them. On this argument also, if he finds any thing ambiguous or obscure in others, he never conceals it. Yet he takes it for granted, that the doctrine which those men oppose has been received without controversy from the remotest antiquity; and yet that he was not uninformed of what others had taught before him, appears even from one word in the first book of his Treatise on the Christian Doctrine, where he says, that unity is in the Father. Will they pretend that he had then forgotten himself? But he elsewhere vindicates himself from this calumny, where he calls the Father the fountain of the whole Deity, because he is from no other; wisely considering that the name of God is especially ascribed to the Father, because, unless the original be from him, it is impossible to conceive of the simple unity of the Deity. These observations, I hope, will be approved by the pious reader, as sufficient to refute all the calumnies, with which Satan has hitherto laboured to pervert or obscure the purity of this doctrine. Finally, I trust that the whole substance of this doctrine has been faithfully stated and explained, provided my readers set bounds to their curiosity, and are not unreasonably fond of tedious and intricate controversies. For I have not the least expectation of giving satisfaction to those who are pleased with an intemperance of speculation. I am sure I have used no artifice in the omission of any thing, from a supposition that it would make against me. But, studying the edification of the Church, I have thought it better not to touch upon many things, which would be unnecessarily burdensome to the reader, without yielding him any profit. For to what purpose is it to dispute, whether the Father be always begetting? For it is foolish to imagine a continual act of generation, since it is evident that three Persons have subsisted in God from all eternity.

6.

The True God Clearly Distinguished in the Scripture from All Fictitious Ones by the Creation of the World.

Although Isaiah brings a just accusation of stupidity against the worshippers of fictitious deities, for not having learned, from the foundations of the earth, and the circuit of the heavens, who was the true God, yet such is the slowness and dulness of our minds, as to induce a necessity for a more express exhibition of the true God, lest the faithful should decline to the fictions of the heathen. For, since the most tolerable description given by the philosophers, that God is the soul of the world, is utterly vain and worthless, we require a more familiar knowledge of him, to prevent us from wavering in perpetual uncertainty. Therefore he hath been pleased to give us a history of the creation, on which the faith of the Church might rest, without seeking after any other God than him whom Moses has represented as the former and builder of the world. The first thing specified in this history is the time, that by a continued series of years the faithful might arrive at the first original of the human race, and of all things. This knowledge is eminently useful, not only to contradict the monstrous fables formerly received in Egypt and other countries, but also to give us clearer views of the eternity of God, and to fill us with greater admiration of it. Nor ought we to be moved with that profane sneer, that it is marvellous that God did not form the design of creating heaven and earth at an earlier period, but suffered an immeasurable duration to pass away unemployed, since he could have made them many thousands of ages before; whereas the continuance of the world, now advancing to its last end, has not yet reached six thousand years. For the reason why God deferred it so long, it would be neither lawful nor expedient to inquire; because, if the human mind strive to penetrate it, it will fail a hundred times in the attempt; nor, indeed, could there be any utility in the knowledge of that which God himself, in order to prove the modesty of our faith, has purposely concealed. Great shrewdness was discovered by a certain pious old man, who, when some scoffer ludicrously inquired what God had been doing before the creation of the world, replied that he had been making hell for over curious men. This admonition, no less grave than severe, should repress the wantonness which stimulates many, and impels them to perverse and injurious speculations. Lastly, let us remember that God, who is invisible, and whose wisdom, power, and justice, are incomprehensible, has placed before us the history of Moses, as a mirror which exhibits his lively image. For as eyes, either dim through age, or dull through any disease, see nothing distinctly without the assistance of spectacles, so, in our inquiries after God, such is our imbecility, without the guidance of the Scripture we immediately lose our way. But those who indulge their presumption, since they are now admonished in vain, will perceive too late, by their horrible destruction, how much better it would have been to look up to the secret counsels of God with reverential awe, than to disgorge their blasphemies to darken the heaven. Augustine justly complains, that it is an offence against God, to inquire for any cause of things, higher than his will. He elsewhere prudently cautions us, that it is as absurd to dispute concerning an infinite duration of time, as concerning an infinite extent of place. However extensive the circuit of the heavens, yet certainly it has some dimensions. Now, if any one should expostulate with God, that the vacuity of space is a hundred times larger, would not such arrogance be detested by all pious persons? The same madness is chargeable on those who censure the inaction of God, for not having, according to their wishes, created the world innumerable ages before. To gratify their inordinate curiosity, they desire to pass beyond the limits of the world; as though, in the very ample circumference of heaven and earth, we were not surrounded by numerous objects capable of absorbing all our senses in their inestimable splendour; as though, in the course of six thousand years, God had not given us lessons sufficient to exercise our minds in assiduous meditation on them. Then let us cheerfully remain within these barriers with which God has been pleased to circumscribe us, and as it were to confine our minds, that they might not be wandering in the boundless regions of uncertain conjecture.

II. To the same purpose is the narration of Moses, that the work of God was completed, not in one moment, but in six days. For by this circumstance also we are called away from all false deities to the only true God, who distributed his work into six days, that it might not be tedious to us to occupy the whole of life in the consideration of it. For though, whithersoever we turn our eyes, they are constrained to behold the works of God, yet we see how transient our attention is, and, if we are touched with any pious reflections, how soon they leave us again. Here, also, human reason murmurs, as though such progressive works were inconsistent with the power of Deity; till, subdued to the obedience of faith, it learns to observe that rest, to which the sanctification of the seventh day invites us. Now, in the order of those things, we must diligently consider the paternal love of God towards the human race, in not creating Adam before he had enriched the earth with an abundant supply of every thing conducive to his happiness. For had he placed him in the earth while it remained barren and vacant, had he given him life before there was any light, he would have appeared not very attentive to his benefit. Now, when he has regulated the motions of the sun and the stars for the service of man, replenished the earth, the air, and the waters, with living creatures, and caused the earth to produce an abundance of all kinds of fruits sufficient for sustenance, he acts the part of a provident and sedulous father of a family, and displays his wonderful goodness towards us. If the reader will more attentively consider with himself these things, which I only hint at as I proceed, he will be convinced that Moses was an authentic witness and herald of the one God, the Creator of the world. I pass over what I have already stated, that he not only speaks of the mere essence of God, but also exhibits to us his eternal Wisdom and his Spirit, in order that we may not dream of any other God except him who will be known in that express image.

III. But before I begin to enlarge on the nature of man, something must be said concerning angels. Because, though Moses, in the history of the creation, accommodating himself to the ignorance of the common people, mentions no other works of God than such as are visible to our eyes, yet, when he afterwards introduces angels as ministers of God, we may easily conclude, that he is their Creator, whom they obey, and in whose service they are employed. Though Moses, therefore, speaking in a popular manner, does not, in the beginning of his writings, immediately enumerate the angels among the creatures of God, yet nothing forbids our here making a plain and explicit statement of those things which the Scripture teaches in other places; because, if we desire to know God from his works, such an excellent and noble specimen should by no means be omitted. Besides, this point of doctrine is very necessary for the confutation of many errors. The excellence of the angelic nature has so dazzled the minds of many, that they have supposed them to be injured, if they were treated as mere creatures, subject to the government of one God. Hence they were falsely pretended to possess a kind of divinity. Manichæus has also arisen, with the sect which he founded, who imagined to himself two original principles, God and the devil; and attributed to God the origin of all good things, but referred evil natures to the production of the devil. If our minds were bewildered in this wild and incoherent system, we should not leave God in full possession of his glory in the creation of the world. For, since nothing is more peculiar to God than eternity and self-existence, does not the ascription of this to the devil dignify him with a title of Divinity? Now, where is the omnipotence of God, if such an empire be conceded to the devil, as that he can execute whatever he pleases, notwithstanding the aversion of the Divine will, or opposition of the Divine power? But the only foundation of the system of Manichæus, that it is unlawful to ascribe to a good God the creation of any evil thing, in no respect affects the orthodox faith, which admits not that any thing in the universe is evil in its nature; since neither the depravity and wickedness of men and devils, nor the sins which proceed from that source, are from mere nature, but from a corruption of nature; nor from the beginning has any thing existed, in which God has not given a specimen both of his wisdom and of his justice. To oppose these perverse notions, it is necessary to raise our minds higher than our eyes can reach. And it is very probable that it was with this design, when, in the Nicene creed, God is called the Creator of all things, that particular mention is made of things invisible. Yet it shall be my study to observe the limit which the rule of piety prescribes, lest, by indulging an unprofitable degree of speculation, I should lead the reader astray from the simplicity of the faith. And certainly, since the Spirit invariably teaches us in a profitable manner, but, with regard to things of little importance to edification, either is wholly silent, or but lightly and cursorily touches on them,—it is also our duty cheerfully to remain in ignorance of what it is not for our advantage to know.

IV. Since angels are ministers of God appointed to execute his commands, that they are also his creatures, ought to be admitted without controversy. And does it not betray obstinacy rather than diligence, to raise any contention concerning the time or the order in which they were created? Moses narrates, that "the heavens and the earth were finished, and all the host of them:" to what purpose is it anxiously to inquire, on what day, besides the stars and the planets, the other more concealed hosts of heaven began to exist? Not to be too prolix, let us remember on this point (as on the whole doctrine of religion) to observe one rule of modesty and sobriety; which is, not to speak, or think, or even desire to know, concerning obscure subjects, any thing beyond the information given us in the Divine word. Another rule to be followed is, in reading the Scripture, continually to direct our attention to investigate and meditate upon things conducive to edification; not to indulge curiosity or the study of things unprofitable. And, since the Lord has been pleased to instruct us, not in frivolous questions, but in solid piety, the fear of his name, true confidence, and the duties of holiness, let us content ourselves with that knowledge. Wherefore, if we wish to be truly wise, we must forsake the vain imaginations propagated by triflers concerning the nature, orders, and multitude of angels. I know that these things are embraced by many persons with greater avidity, and dwelt upon with more pleasure, than such things as are in daily use. But, if it be not irksome to be the disciples of Christ, it should not be irksome to follow that method which he has prescribed. Then the consequence will be, that, content with his discipline, we shall not only leave, but also abhor, those unprofitable speculations from which he calls us away. No man can deny that great subtlety and acuteness is discovered by Dionysius, whoever he was, in many parts of his treatise on the Celestial Hierarchy; but, if any one enters into a critical examination of it, he will find the greatest part of it to be mere babbling. But the duty of a theologian is, not to please the ear with empty sounds, but to confirm the conscience by teaching things which are true, certain, and profitable. A reader of that book would suppose that the author was a man descended from heaven, giving an account of things that he had not learned from the information of others, but had seen with his own eyes. But Paul, who was "caught up to the third heaven," not only has told us no such things, but has even declared, that it is not lawful for men to utter the secret things which he had seen. Taking our leave, therefore, of this nugatory wisdom, let us consider, from the simple doctrine of the Scripture, what the Lord has been pleased for us to know concerning his angels.

V. We are frequently informed in the Scripture, that angels are celestial spirits, whose ministry and service God uses for the execution of whatever he has decreed; and hence this name is given to them, because God employs them as messengers to manifest himself to men. Other appellations also, by which they are distinguished, are derived from a similar cause. They are called Hosts, because, as life-guards, they surround their prince, aggrandizing his majesty, and rendering it conspicuous; and, like soldiers, are ever attentive to the signal of their leader; and are so prepared for the performance of his commands, that he has no sooner signified his will than they are ready for the work, or rather are actually engaged in it. Such a representation of the throne of God is exhibited in the magnificent descriptions of the Prophets, but particularly of Daniel; where he says, when God had ascended the judgment-seat, that "thousand thousands ministered unto him, and ten thousand times ten thousand stood before him." Since by their means the Lord wonderfully exerts and declares the power and strength of his hand, thence they are denominated Powers. Because by them he exercises and administers his government in the world, therefore they are called sometimes Principalities, sometimes Powers, sometimes Dominions. Lastly, because the glory of God in some measure resides in them, they have also, for this reason, the appellation of Thrones; although on this last name I would affirm nothing, because a different interpretation is equally or even more suitable. But, omitting this name, the Holy Spirit often uses the former ones, to magnify the dignity of the angelic ministry. Nor, indeed, is it right that no honour should be paid to those instruments, by whom God particularly exhibits the presence of his power. Moreover, they are more than once called gods; because in their ministry, as in a mirror, they give us an imperfect representation of Divinity. Though I am pleased with the interpretation of the old writers, on those passages where the Scripture records the appearance of an angel of God to Abraham, Jacob, Moses, and others, that Christ was that angel, yet frequently, where mention is made of angels in general, this name is given to them. Nor should this surprise us; for, if that honour be given to princes and governors, because, in the performance of their functions, they are vicegerents of God, the supreme King and Judge, there is far greater reason for its being paid to angels, in whom the splendour of the Divine glory is far more abundantly displayed.

VI. But the Scripture principally insists on what might conduce most to our consolation, and the confirmation of our faith—that the angels are the dispensers and administrators of the Divine beneficence towards us; and therefore it informs us, that they guard our safety, undertake our defence, direct our ways, and exercise a constant solicitude that no evil befall us. The declarations are universal, belonging primarily to Christ the head of the Church, and then to all the faithful: "He shall give his angels charge over thee, to keep thee in all thy ways. They shall bear thee up in their hands, lest thou dash thy foot against a stone." Again, "The angel of the Lord encampeth round about them that fear him, and delivereth them." In these passages God shows that he delegates to his angels the protection of those whom he has undertaken to preserve. Accordingly, the angel of the Lord consoles the fugitive Hagar, and commands her to be reconciled to her mistress. Abraham promises his servant that an angel should be the guide of his journey. Jacob, in his benediction of Ephraim and Manasseh, prays that the angel of the Lord, by whom he had been redeemed from all evil, would cause them to prosper. Thus an angel was appointed to protect the camp of the Israelites; and whenever it pleased God to deliver them from the hands of their enemies, he raised up avengers by the ministry of angels. And finally, to supersede the necessity of adducing more examples, angels ministered to Christ and attended him in all his difficulties; they announced his resurrection to the women, and his glorious advent to the disciples. And thus, in the discharge of their office as our protectors, they contend against the devil and all our enemies, and execute the vengeance of God on those who molest us; as we read that an angel of God, to deliver Jerusalem from a siege, slew a hundred and eighty-five thousand men in the camp of the king of Assyria in one night.

VII. But whether each of the faithful has a particular angel assigned him for his defence, I cannot venture certainly to affirm. When Daniel introduces the angel of the Persians and the angel of the Greeks, he clearly signifies that certain angels are appointed to preside over kingdoms and provinces. Christ also, when he says that the angels of children always behold the face of the Father, suggests, that there are certain angels who are charged with their safety. But I know not whether this justifies the conclusion, that every one of them has his particular guardian angel. Of this, indeed, we may be certain, that not one angel only has the care of every one of us, but that they all with one consent watch for our salvation. For it is said of all the angels together, that they rejoice more over one sinner turned to repentance, than over ninety and nine just persons who have persevered in their righteousness. Of more than one angel it is said, that they carried the soul of Lazarus into the bosom of Abraham. Nor is it in vain that Elisha shows his servant so many fiery chariots, which were peculiarly assigned to him for his protection. There is one place which seems clearer than the rest in confirmation of this point. For when Peter, on his liberation from prison, knocked at the door of the house in which the brethren were assembled, as they could not suppose it to be Peter himself, they said it was his angel. This conclusion seems to have arisen in their minds from the common opinion that each of the faithful has his guardian angel assigned him. But here it may also be replied, that nothing prevents this being understood of any one of the angels, to whom the Lord might have committed the care of Peter on that occasion, and who yet might not be his perpetual guardian; as it is vulgarly imagined that every person has two angels, a good one and a bad one, according to the heathen notion of different genii. But it is not worth while anxiously to investigate what it little concerns us to know. For if any one be not satisfied with this, that all the orders of the celestial army watch for his safety, I see not what advantage he can derive from knowing that he has one particular angel given him for his guardian. But those who restrict to one angel the care which God exercises over every one of us, do a great injury to themselves, and to all the members of the Church; as though those auxiliaries had been promised in vain, who, by surrounding and defending us on all sides, contribute to increase our courage in the conflict.

VIII. Let those, who venture to determine concerning the multitude and orders of the angels, examine on what foundation their opinions rest. Michael, I confess, is called in Daniel "the great prince," and in Jude "the archangel." And Paul informs us that it will be an archangel, who, with the sound of a trumpet, shall summon men to judgment. But who, from these passages, can determine the degrees of honour among the angels, distinguish the individuals by their respective titles, and assign to every one his place and station? For the two names which are found in the Scripture, Michael and Gabriel, and the third, if you wish to add it from the history of Tobias, may appear, from their significations, to be given to angels on account of our infirmity; though I would rather leave this undetermined. With respect to their numbers, we hear, from the mouth of Christ, of many legions; from Daniel, of many myriads: the servant of Elisha saw many chariots; and their being said to encamp round about them that fear God, is expressive of a great multitude. It is certain that spirits have no form; and yet the Scripture, on account of the slender capacity of our minds, under the names of cherubim and seraphim, represents angels to us as having wings, to prevent our doubting that they will always attend, with incredible celerity, to afford us assistance as soon as our cases require it; as though the lightning darted from heaven were to fly to us with its accustomed velocity. All further inquiries on both these points, we should consider as belonging to that class of mysteries, the full revelation of which is deferred to the last day. Wherefore let us remember that we ought to avoid too much curiosity of research, and presumption of language.

IX. But this, which is called in question by some restless men, must be received as a certain truth, that angels are ministering spirits, whose service God uses for the protection of his people, and by whom he dispenses his benefits among mankind, and executes his other works. It was the opinion of the ancient Sadducees, indeed, that the term *angels* signified nothing but the motions which God inspires into men, or those specimens which he gives of his power. But this foolish notion is repugnant to so many testimonies of Scripture, that it is surprising how such gross ignorance could have been tolerated among that people. For, to omit the places before cited, where mention is made of thousands and legions of angels; where joy is attributed to them; where they are said to sustain the faithful in their hands, to carry their souls into rest, to behold the face of the Father, and the like,—there are others which most clearly evince, that they are spirits possessing an actual existence and their own peculiar nature. For the declarations of Stephen and Paul,—that the law was given by the hand of angels, and of Christ, that the elect, after the resurrection, shall be like angels; that the day of judgment is not known even to the angels; that he then will come with his holy angels,—however tortured, must necessarily be thus understood. Likewise, when Paul charges Timothy, before Christ and the elect angels, to keep his precepts, he intends, not unsubstantial qualities or inspirations, but real spirits. Nor otherwise is there any meaning in what we read in the Epistle to the Hebrews, that Christ is made more excellent than the angels, that the world is not subject to them, that Christ assumed not their nature, but the nature of man, unless we understand that there are happy spirits, to whom these comparisons may apply. And the author of the same epistle explains himself, where he places angels and the souls of the faithful together in the kingdom of God. Besides, we have already quoted, that the angels of children always behold the face of God; that we are always defended by their protection; that they rejoice for our safety; that they admire the manifold grace of God in the church; and are subject to Christ as their head. The same truth is proved by their having so often appeared to the patriarchs in the form of men, conversed with them, and been entertained by them. And Christ himself, on account of the preëminence which he obtains in the capacity of Mediator, is called an angel. I have thought proper cursorily to touch on this point, in order to fortify the simple against those foolish and absurd notions, which were disseminated by Satan many ages ago, and are frequently springing up afresh.

X. It remains for us to encounter the superstition, which generally insinuates itself into men's minds when angels are said to be the ministers and dispensers of all our blessings. For human reason soon falls into an opinion, that there is no honour that ought not to be paid to them. Thus it happens that what belongs solely to God and Christ, is transferred to them. Thus we see, that for some ages past the glory of Christ has in many ways been obscured; while angels have been loaded with extravagant honours without the authority of the word of God. And among the errors which we combat in the present day, there is scarcely one more ancient than this. For even Paul appears to have had a great controversy with some, who exalted angels in such a manner as almost to degrade Christ to an inferior station. Hence the solicitude with which he maintains, in the Epistle to the Colossians, not only that Christ is to be esteemed above angels, but also that he is the author of all blessings to them, in order that we may not forsake him and turn to them, who are not even sufficient for themselves, but draw from the same fountain as we do. Since the splendour of the Divine majesty, therefore, is eminently displayed in them, there is nothing more natural than for us to fall down with astonishment in adoration of them, and to attribute every thing to them which exclusively belongs to God. Even John, in the Revelation, confesses this to have happened to himself; but adds at the same time, that he was thus answered: "See thou do it not: I am thy fellow-servant: worship God."

XI. But this danger we shall happily avoid, if we consider why God is accustomed to provide for the safety of the faithful, and to communicate the gifts of his beneficence by means of angels, rather than by himself to manifest his own power without their intervention. He certainly does this not from necessity, as though he were unable to do without them; for whenever he pleases he passes them by, and performs his work with a mere nod of his power; so far is he from being indebted to their assistance for relieving him in any difficulty. This, therefore, conduces to the consolation of our imbecility, that we may want nothing that can either raise our minds to a good hope, or confirm them in security. This one thing, indeed, ought to be more than sufficient for us, that the Lord declares himself to be our Protector. But while we see ourselves encompassed with so many dangers, so many annoyances, such various kinds of enemies,—such is our weakness and frailty, that we may sometimes be filled with terror, or fall into despair, unless the Lord enables us, according to our capacity, to discover the presence of his grace. For this reason he promises, not only that he will take care of us himself, but also that we shall have innumerable life-guards, to whom he has committed the charge of our safety; and that, as long as we are surrounded by their superintendence and protection, whatever danger may threaten, we are placed beyond the utmost reach of evil. I confess, indeed, that it is wrong for us, after that simple promise of the protection of God alone, still to be looking around to see from what quarter our aid may come. But since the Lord, from his infinite clemency and goodness, is pleased to assist this our weakness, there is no reason why we should neglect this great favour which he shows us. We have an example of this in the servant of Elisha, who, when he saw that the mountain was besieged by an army of Syrians, and that no way of escape was left, was filled with consternation, as though himself and his master had been ruined. Then Elisha prayed that God would open his eyes, and he immediately saw the mountain full of horses and chariots of fire; that is, of a multitude of angels who were to guard him and the Prophet. Encouraged by this vision, he came to himself again, and was able to look down with intrepidity on the enemies, the sight of whom before had almost deprived him of life.

XII. Therefore, whatever is said concerning the ministry of angels, let us direct it to this end, that, overcoming all diffidence, our hope in God may be more firmly established. For the Lord has provided these guards for us, that we may not be terrified by a multitude of enemies, as though they could prevail in opposition to his assistance, but may have recourse to the sentiment expressed by Elisha, "There are more for us than against us." How preposterous is it, then, that we should be alienated from God by angels, who are appointed for this very purpose, to testify that his aid is more especially present with us! But they do alienate us from him, unless they lead us directly to him, to regard him, call on him, and celebrate him as our only helper; unless they are considered by us as his hands, which apply themselves to do nothing without his direction; unless they attach us to Christ, the only Mediator, to depend entirely on him, to lean upon him, to aspire to him, and to rest satisfied in him. For what is described in the vision of Jacob ought to be firmly fixed in our minds, that the angels descend to the earth to men, and ascend from earth to heaven, by a ladder above which stands the Lord of hosts. This implies, that it is only through the intercession of Christ, that we are favoured with the ministry of angels, as he himself affirms: "Hereafter ye shall see heaven open, and the angels descending upon the Son of man." Therefore the servant of Abraham, having been commended to the care of an angel, does not therefore invoke him for his aid, but, trusting to that committal, pours out his prayers before the Lord, and entreats him to display his mercy towards Abraham. For as God does not make them the ministers of his power and goodness, in order to divide his glory with them, so neither does he promise his assistance in their ministry, that we may divide our confidence between them and him. Let us take our leave, therefore, of that Platonic philosophy, which seeks access to God by means of angels, and worships them in order to render him more propitious to us; which superstitious and curious men have endeavoured from the beginning, and even to this day persevere in attempting, to introduce into our religion.

XIII. The design of almost every thing that the Scripture teaches concerning devils, is that we may be careful to guard against their insidious machinations, and may provide ourselves with such weapons as are sufficiently firm and strong to repel the most powerful enemies. For when Satan is called the god and prince of this world, the strong man armed, the prince of the power of the air, a roaring lion, these descriptions only tend to make us more cautious and vigilant, and better prepared to encounter him. This is sometimes signified in express words. For Peter, after having said that "the devil, as a roaring lion, walketh about seeking whom he may devour," immediately subjoins an exhortation to "resist him, steadfast in the faith." And Paul, having suggested that "we wrestle not against flesh and blood, but against principalities, against powers, against the rulers of the darkness of this world, against spiritual wickedness," immediately commands us to put on suitable armour for so great and so perilous a conflict. Wherefore, having been previously warned that we are perpetually threatened by an enemy, and an enemy desperately bold and extremely strong, skilled in every artifice, indefatigable in diligence and celerity, abundantly provided with all kinds of weapons, and most expert in the science of war, let us make it the grand object of our attention, that we suffer not ourselves to be oppressed with slothfulness and inactivity, but, on the contrary, arousing and collecting all our courage, be ready for a vigorous resistance; and as this warfare is terminated only by death, let us encourage ourselves to perseverance. But, above all, conscious of weakness and ignorance, let us implore the assistance of God, nor attempt any thing but in reliance on him; since he alone can supply us with wisdom, and strength, and courage, and armour.

XIV. But, the more to excite and urge us to such conduct, the Scripture announces that there are not one, or two, or a few enemies, but great armies who wage war against us. For even Mary Magdalene is said to have been delivered from seven demons, by whom she was possessed; and Christ declares it to be a common case, that, if you leave the place open for the re-entrance of a demon who has once been ejected, he associates with himself seven spirits more wicked still, and returns to his vacant possession. Indeed, one man is said to have been possessed by a whole legion. By these passages, therefore, we are taught, that we have to contend with an infinite multitude of enemies; lest, despising their paucity, we should be more remiss to encounter them, or, expecting sometimes an intermission of hostility, should indulge ourselves in idleness. But when one Satan or devil is frequently mentioned in the singular number, it denotes that principality of wickedness which opposes the kingdom of righteousness. For as the Church and society of saints have Christ as their head, so the faction of the impious, and impiety itself, are represented to us with their prince, who exercises the supreme power among them; which is the meaning of that sentence, "Depart, ye cursed, into everlasting fire, prepared for the devil and his angels."

XV. It also ought to stimulate us to a perpetual war with the devil, that he is every where called God's adversary and ours. For, if we feel the concern which we ought to feel for the glory of God, we shall exert all our power against him who attempts the extinction of it. If we are animated by a becoming zeal for defending the kingdom of Christ, we must necessarily have an irreconcilable war with him who conspires its ruin. On the other hand, if we are solicitous for our salvation, we ought to make neither peace nor truce with him who assiduously plots its destruction. Now, such is the description given of him in the third chapter of Genesis, where he seduces man from the obedience owed by him to God, so that he at once robs God of his just honour, and precipitates man into ruin. Such, also, is he described in the Evangelists, where he is called an enemy, and said to sow tares in order to corrupt the seed of eternal life. In short, the testimony of Christ concerning him, that he was a murderer and a liar from the beginning, we find verified in all his actions. For he opposes Divine truth with lies; obscures the light with shades of darkness; involves the minds of men in errors; stirs up animosities, and kindles contentions and wars;—and all for the purpose of subverting the kingdom of God, and plunging mankind with himself into eternal destruction. Whence it is evident, that he is naturally depraved, vicious, malignant, and mischievous. For there must be extreme depravity in that mind which is bent on opposing the glory of God and the salvation of men. And this is suggested by John in his Epistle, when he says, that "he sinneth from the beginning." For he intends, that he is the author, conductor, and principal contriver of all wickedness and iniquity.

XVI. But since the devil was created by God, we must remark, that this wickedness which we attribute to his nature is not from creation, but from corruption. For whatever evil quality he has, he has acquired by his defection and fall. And of this the Scripture apprizes us; lest, believing him to have come from God, just as he now is, we should ascribe to God himself that which is in direct opposition to him. For this reason Christ declares, that Satan, "when he speaketh a lie, speaketh of his own;" and adds the reason—"because he abode not in the truth." When he says that he abode not in the truth, he certainly implies that he had once been in it; and when he calls him the father of a lie, he precludes his imputing to God the depravity of his nature, which originated wholly from himself. Though these things are delivered in a brief and rather obscure manner, yet they are abundantly sufficient to vindicate the majesty of God from every calumny. And what does it concern us to know, respecting devils, either more particulars, or for any other purpose? Some persons are displeased that the Scripture does not give us, in various places, a distinct and detailed account of their fall, with its cause, manner, time, and nature. But, these things being nothing to us, it was better for them, if not to be passed over in total silence, yet certainly to be touched on but lightly; because it would ill comport with the dignity of the Holy Spirit to feed curiosity with vain and unprofitable histories; and we perceive it to have been the design of the Lord, to deliver nothing in his sacred oracles, which we might not learn to our edification. That we ourselves, therefore, may not dwell upon unprofitable subjects, let us be content with this concise information respecting the nature of devils; that at their creation they were originally angels of God, but by degenerating have ruined themselves, and become the instruments of perdition to others. This being useful to be known, it is clearly stated by Peter and Jude. "God," say they, "spared not the angels that sinned, and kept not their first estate, but left their own habitation." And Paul, mentioning the elect angels, without doubt tacitly implies that there are reprobate ones.

XVII. The discord and contention, which we say Satan maintains against God, ought to be understood in a manner consistent with a firm persuasion, that he can do nothing without God's will and consent. For we read in the history of Job, that he presented himself before God to receive his commands, and dared not to undertake any enterprise without having obtained his permission. Thus, also, when Ahab was to be deceived, he undertook to be a lying spirit in the mouth of all the prophets; and, being commissioned by God, he performed it. For this reason he is also called the "evil spirit from the Lord," who tormented Saul, because he was employed as a scourge to punish the sins of that impious monarch. And elsewhere it is recorded, that the plagues were inflicted on the Egyptians by the "evil angels." According to these particular examples, Paul declares generally, that the blinding of unbelievers is the work of God, whereas he had before called it the operation of Satan. It appears, then, that Satan is subject to the power of God, and so governed by his control, that he is compelled to render obedience to him. Now, when we say that Satan resists God, and that his works are contrary to the works of God, we at the same time assert that this repugnance and contention depend on the Divine permission. I speak now, not of the will or the endeavour, but only of the effect. For the devil, being naturally wicked, has not the least inclination towards obedience to the Divine will, but is wholly bent on insolence and rebellion. It therefore arises from himself and his wickedness, that he opposes God with all his desires and purposes. This depravity stimulates him to attempt those things which he thinks the most opposed to God. But since God holds him tied and bound with the bridle of his power, he executes only those things which are divinely permitted; and thus, whether he will or not, he obeys his Creator, being constrained to fulfil any service to which he impels him.

XVIII. While God directs the courses of unclean spirits hither and thither at his pleasure, he regulates this government in such a manner, that they exercise the faithful with fighting, attack them in ambuscades, harass them with incursions, push them in battles, and frequently fatigue them, throw them into confusion, terrify them, and sometimes wound them, yet never conquer or overwhelm them; but subdue and lead captive the impious, tyrannize over their souls and bodies, and abuse them like slaves by employing them in the perpetration of every enormity. The faithful, in consequence of being harassed by such enemies, are addressed with the following, and other similar exhortations: "Give not place to the devil." "Your adversary the devil, as a roaring lion, walketh about, seeking whom he may devour; whom resist, steadfast in the faith." Paul confesses that he himself was not free from this kind of warfare, when he declares that, as a remedy to subdue pride, "the messenger of Satan was given to him to buffet him." This exercise, then, is common to all the children of God. But, as the promise respecting the breaking of the head of Satan belongs to Christ and all his members in common, I therefore deny that the faithful can ever be conquered or overwhelmed by him. They are frequently filled with consternation, but recover themselves again; they fall by the violence of his blows, but are raised up again; they are wounded, but not mortally; finally, they labour through their whole lives in such a manner, as at last to obtain the victory. This, however, is not to be restricted to each single action. For we know that, by the righteous vengeance of God, David was for a time delivered to Satan, that by his instigation he might number the people; nor is it without reason that Paul admits a hope of pardon even for those who may have been entangled in the snares of the devil. Therefore the same Apostle shows, in another place, that the promise before cited is begun in this life, where we must engage in the conflict; and that after the termination of the conflict it will be completed. "And the God of peace," he says, "shall bruise Satan under your feet shortly." In our Head this victory, indeed, has always been complete, because the prince of this world had nothing in him: in us, who are his members, it yet appears only in part, but will be completed when we shall have put off our flesh, which makes us still subject to infirmities, and shall be full of the power of the Holy Spirit. In this manner, when the kingdom of Christ is erected, Satan and his power must fall; as the Lord himself says, "I beheld Satan as lightning falling from heaven." For by this answer he confirms what the Apostles had reported concerning the power of his preaching. Again: "When a strong man armed keepeth his palace, his goods are in peace; but when a stronger than he shall come upon him and overcome him," &c. And to this end Christ by his death overcame Satan, who had the power of death, and triumphed over all his forces, that they might not be able to hurt the Church; for otherwise it would be in hourly danger of destruction. For such is our imbecility, and such the strength of his fury, how could we stand even for a moment against his various and unceasing attacks, without being supported by the victory of our Captain? Therefore God permits not Satan to exercise any power over the souls of the faithful, but abandons to his government only the impious and unbelieving, whom he designs not to number among his own flock. For he is said to have the undisturbed possession of this world, till he is expelled by Christ. He is said also to blind all who believe not the Gospel, and to work in the children of disobedience; and this justly, for all the impious are vessels of wrath. To whom, therefore, should they be subjected, but to the minister of the Divine vengeance? Finally, they are said to be of their father the devil; because, as the faithful are known to be the children of God from their bearing his image, so the impious, from the image of Satan into which they have degenerated, are properly considered as his children.

XIX. But as we have already confuted that nugatory philosophy concerning the holy angels, which teaches that they are nothing but inspirations, or good motions, excited by God in the minds of men, so in this place we must refute those who pretend that devils are nothing but evil affections or perturbations, which our flesh obtrudes on our minds. But this may be easily done, and that because the testimonies of Scripture on this subject are numerous and clear. First, when they are called unclean spirits and apostate angels, who have degenerated from their original condition, the very names sufficiently express, not mental emotions or affections, but rather in reality what are called minds, or spirits endued with perception and intelligence. Likewise, when the children of God are compared with the children of the devil, both by Christ and by John, would not the comparison be absurd, if nothing were intended by the word *devil* but evil inspirations? And John adds something still plainer, that the devil sins from the beginning. Likewise, when Jude introduces Michael the archangel contending with the devil, he certainly opposes to the good angel an evil and rebellious one; to which agrees what is recorded in the history of Job, that Satan appeared with the holy angels before God. But the clearest of all are those passages, which mention the punishment which they begin to feel from the judgment of God, and are to feel much more at the resurrection: "Thou Son of God, art thou come hither to torment us before the time?" Also, "Depart, ye cursed, into everlasting fire, prepared for the devil and his angels." Again, "If God spared not the angels that sinned, but cast them down to hell, and delivered them into chains of darkness, to be reserved unto judgment," &c. How unmeaning were these expressions, that the devils are appointed to eternal judgment; that fire is prepared for them; that they are now tormented and vexed by the glory of Christ, if there were no devils at all! But since this point is not a subject of dispute with those who give credit to the word of the Lord, but with those vain speculators who are pleased with nothing but novelty, little good can be effected by testimonies of Scripture. I consider myself as having done what I intended, which was to fortify the pious mind against such a species of errors, with which restless men disturb themselves and others that are more simple. But it was requisite to touch on it, lest any persons involved in that error, under a supposition that they have no adversary, should become more slothful and incautious to resist him.

XX. Yet let us not disdain to receive a pious delight from the works of God, which every where present themselves to view in this very beautiful theatre of the world.

For this, as I have elsewhere observed, though not the principal, is yet, in the order of nature, the first lesson of faith, to remember that, whithersoever we turn our eyes, all the things which we behold are the works of God; and at the same time to consider, with pious meditation, for what end God created them. Therefore to apprehend, by a true faith, what it is for our benefit to know concerning God, we must first of all understand the history of the creation of the world, as it is briefly related by Moses, and afterwards more copiously illustrated by holy men, particularly by Basil and Ambrose. Thence we shall learn that God, by the power of his Word and Spirit, created out of nothing the heaven and the earth; that from them he produced all things, animate and inanimate; distinguished by an admirable gradation the innumerable variety of things; to every species gave its proper nature, assigned its offices, and appointed its places and stations; and since all things are subject to corruption, has, nevertheless, provided for the preservation of every species till the last day; that he therefore nourishes some by methods concealed from us, from time to time infusing, as it were, new vigour into them; that on some he has conferred the power of propagation, in order that the whole species may not be extinct at their death; that he has thus wonderfully adorned heaven and earth with the utmost possible abundance, variety, and beauty, like a large and splendid mansion, most exquisitely and copiously furnished; lastly, that, by creating man, and distinguishing him with such splendid beauty, and with such numerous and great privileges, he has exhibited in him a most excellent specimen of all his works. But since it is not my design to treat at large of the creation of the world, let it suffice to have again dropped these few hints by the way. For it is better, as I have just advised the reader, to seek for fuller information on this subject from Moses, and others who have faithfully and diligently recorded the history of the world.

XXI. It is useless to enter into a prolix disputation respecting the right tendency and legitimate design of a consideration of the works of God, since this question has been, in a great measure, determined in another place, and, as much as concerns our present purpose, may be despatched in few words. Indeed, if we wished to explain how the inestimable wisdom, power, justice, and goodness, of God are manifested in the formation of the world, no splendour or ornament of diction will equal the magnitude of so great a subject. And it is undoubtedly the will of the Lord, that we should be continually employed in this holy meditation; that, while we contemplate in all the creatures, as in so many mirrors, the infinite riches of his wisdom, justice, goodness, and power, we might not only take a transient and cursory view of them, but might long dwell on the idea, seriously and faithfully revolve it in our minds, and frequently recall it to our memory. But, this being a didactic treatise, we must omit those topics which require long declamations. To be brief, therefore, let the readers know, that they have then truly apprehended by faith what is meant by God being the Creator of heaven and earth, if they, in the first place, follow this universal rule, not to pass over, with ungrateful inattention or oblivion, those glorious perfections which God manifests in his creatures; and, secondly, learn to make such an application to themselves as thoroughly to affect their hearts. The first point is exemplified, when we consider how great must have been the Artist who disposed that multitude of stars, which adorn the heaven, in such a regular order, that it is impossible to imagine any thing more beautiful to behold; who fixed some in their stations, so that they cannot be moved; who granted to others a freer course, but so that they never travel beyond their appointed limits; who so regulates the motions of all, that they measure days and nights, months, years, and seasons of the year; and also reduces the inequality of days, which we constantly witness, to such a medium that it occasions no confusion. So, also, when we observe his power in sustaining so great a mass, in governing the rapid revolutions of the celestial machine, and the like. For these few examples sufficiently declare, what it is to recognize the perfections of God in the creation of the world. Otherwise, were I desirous of pursuing the subject to its full extent, there would be no end; since there are as many miracles of Divine power, as many monuments of Divine goodness, as many proofs of Divine wisdom, as there are species of things in the world, and even as there are individual things, either great or small.

XXII. There remains the other point, which approaches more nearly to faith; that, while we observe how God has appointed all things for our benefit and safety, and at the same time perceive his power and grace in ourselves, and the great benefits which he has conferred on us, we may thence excite ourselves to confide in him, to invoke him, to praise him, and to love him. Now, as I have just before suggested, God himself has demonstrated, by the very order of creation, that he made all things for the sake of man. For it was not without reason that he distributed the making of the world into six days; though it would have been no more difficult for him to complete the whole work, in all its parts, at once, in a single moment, than to arrive at its completion by such progressive advances. But in this he has been pleased to display his providence and paternal solicitude towards us, since, before he would make man, he prepared every thing which he foresaw would be useful or beneficial to him. How great would be, now, the ingratitude to doubt whether we are regarded by this best of fathers, whom we perceive to have been solicitous on our account before we existed! How impious would it be to tremble with diffidence, lest at any time his benignity should desert us in our necessities, which we see was displayed in the greatest affluence of all blessings provided for us while we were yet unborn! Besides, we are told by Moses, that his liberality has subjected to us all that is contained in the whole world. He certainly has not made this declaration in order to tantalize us with the empty name of such a donation. Therefore we never shall be destitute of any thing which will conduce to our welfare. Finally, to conclude, whenever we call God the Creator of heaven and earth, let us at the same time reflect, that the dispensation of all those things which he has made is in his own power, and that we are his children, whom he has received into his charge and custody, to be supported and educated; so that we may expect every blessing from him alone, and cherish a certain hope that he will never suffer us to want those things which are necessary to our well-being, that our hope may depend on no other; that, whatever we need or desire, our prayers may be directed to him, and that, from whatever quarter we receive any advantage, we may acknowledge it to be his benefit, and confess it with thanksgiving; that, being allured with such great sweetness of goodness and beneficence, we may study to love and worship him with all our hearts.

7.

The Guidance and Teaching of the Scripture Necessary to Lead to the Knowledge of God the Creator.

Though the light which presents itself to all eyes, both in heaven and in earth, is more than sufficient to deprive the ingratitude of men of every excuse, since God, in order to involve all mankind in the same guilt, sets before them all, without exception, an exhibition of his majesty, delineated in the creatures, —yet we need another and better assistance, properly to direct us to the Creator of the world. Therefore, he hath not unnecessarily added the light of his word, to make himself known unto salvation, and hath honored with this privilege those whom he intended to unite in a more close and familiar connection with himself. For, seeing the minds of all men to be agitated with unstable dispositions, when he had chosen the Jews as his peculiar flock, he enclosed them as in a fold, that they might not wander after the vanities of other nations. And it is not without cause that he preserves us in the pure knowledge of himself by the same means; for, otherwise, they who seem comparatively to stand firm, would soon fall. For, as persons who are old, or whose eyes are by any means become dim, if you show them the most beautiful book, though they perceive something written, but can scarcely read two words together, yet, by the assistance of spectacles, will begin to read distinctly, —so the Scripture, collecting in our minds the otherwise confused notions of Deity, dispels the darkness, and gives us a clear view of the true God. This, then, is a singular favour, that, in the instruction of the Church, God not only uses mute teachers, but even opens his own sacred mouth; not only proclaims that some god ought to be worshipped, but at the same time pronounces himself to be the Being to whom this worship is due; and not only teaches the elect to raise their view to a Deity, but also exhibits himself as the object of their contemplation. This method he hath observed toward his Church from the beginning; beside those common lessons of instruction, to afford them also his word; which furnishes a more correct and certain criterion to distinguish him from all fictitious deities. And it was undoubtedly by this assistance that Adam, Noah, Abraham, and the rest of the patriarchs, attained to that familiar knowledge which distinguished them from unbelievers. I speak not yet of the peculiar doctrine of faith which illuminated them into the hope of eternal life. For, to pass from death to life, they must have known God, not only as the Creator, but also as the Redeemer; as they certainly obtained both from his word. For that species of knowledge, which related to him as the Creator and Governor of the world, in order, preceded the other. To this was afterwards added the other internal knowledge, which alone vivifies dead souls, and apprehends God, not only as the Creator of the world, and as the sole Author and Arbiter of all events, but also as the Redeemer in the person of the Mediator. But, being not yet come to the fall of man and the corruption of nature, I also forbear to treat of the remedy. Let the reader remember, therefore, that I am not yet treating of that covenant by which God adopted the children of Abraham, and of that point of doctrine by which believers have always been particularly separated from the profane nations, since that is founded on Christ; but am only showing how we ought to learn from the Scripture, that God, who created the world, may be certainly distinguished from the whole multitude of fictitious deities. The series of subjects will, in due time, lead us to redemption. But, though we shall adduce many testimonies from the New Testament, and some also from the Law and the Prophets, in which Christ is expressly mentioned, yet they will all tend to prove, that the Scripture discovers God to us as the Creator of the world, and declares what sentiments we should form of him, that we may not be seeking after a deity in a labyrinth of uncertainty.

II. But, whether God revealed himself to the patriarchs by oracles and visions, or suggested, by means of the ministry of men, what should be handed down by tradition to their posterity, it is beyond a doubt that their minds were impressed with a firm assurance of the doctrine, so that they were persuaded and convinced that the information they had received came from God. For God always secured to his word an undoubted credit, superior to all human opinion. At length, that the truth might remain in the world in a continual course of instruction to all ages, he determined that the same oracles which he had deposited with the patriarchs should be committed to public records. With this design the Law was promulgated, to which the Prophets were afterwards annexed, as its interpreters.—For, though the uses of the law were many, as will be better seen in the proper place; and particularly the intention of Moses, and of all the prophets, was to teach the mode of reconciliation between God and man, (whence also Paul calls Christ "the end of the law,")—yet I repeat again, that, beside the peculiar doctrine of faith and repentance, which proposes Christ as the Mediator, the Scripture distinguishes the only true God by certain characters and titles, as the Creator and Governor of the world, that he may not be confounded with the multitude of false gods. Therefore, though every man should seriously apply himself to a consideration of the works of God, being placed in this very splendid theatre to be a spectator of them, yet he ought principally to attend to the word, that he may attain superior advantages. And, therefore, it is not surprising, that they who are born in darkness grow more and more hardened in their stupidity; since very few attends to the word of God with teachable dispositions, to restrain themselves within the limits which it prescribes, but rather exult in their own vanity. This, then, must be considered as a fixed principle, that, in order to enjoy the light of true religion, we ought to begin with the doctrine of heaven; and that no man can have the least knowledge of true and sound doctrine, without having been a disciple of the Scripture. Hence originates all true wisdom, when we embrace with reverence the testimony which God hath been pleased therein to deliver concerning himself. For obedience is the source, not only of an absolutely perfect and complete faith, but of all right knowledge of God. And truly in this instance God hath, in his providence, particularly consulted the true interests of mankind in all ages.

III. For, if we consider the mutability of the human mind,—how easy its lapse into forgetfulness of God; how great its propensity to errors of every kind; how violent its rage for the perpetual fabrication of new and false religions,—it will be easy to perceive the necessity of the heavenly doctrine being thus committed to writing, that it might not be lost in oblivion, or evaporate in error, or be corrupted by the presumption of men. Since it is evident, therefore, that God, foreseeing the inefficacy of his manifestation of himself in the exquisite structure of the world, hath afforded the assistance of his word to all those to whom he determined to make his instructions effectual,—if we seriously aspire to a sincere contemplation of God, it is necessary for us to pursue this right way. We must come, I say, to the word, which contains a just and lively description of God as he appears in his works, when those works are estimated, not according to our depraved judgment, but by the rule of eternal truth. If we deviate from it, as I have just observed, though we run with the utmost celerity, yet, being out of the course, we shall never reach the goal. For it must be concluded, that the light of the Divine countenance, which even the Apostle says "no man can approach unto," is like an inexplicable labyrinth to us, unless we are directed by the line of the word; so that it were better to halt in this way, than to run with the greatest rapidity out of it. Therefore David, inculcating the necessity of the removal of superstitions out of the world, that pure religion may flourish, frequently introduces God as "reigning;" by the word "reigning," intending, not the power which he possesses, and which he exercises in the universal government of nature, but the doctrine in which he asserts his legitimate sovereignty; because errors can never be eradicated from the human heart, till the true knowledge of God is implanted in it.

IV. Therefore the same Psalmist, having said, that "the heavens declare the glory of God, and the firmament showeth his handy-work; day unto day uttereth speech, and night unto night showeth knowledge," afterwards proceeds to the mention of the word: "The law of the Lord is perfect, converting the soul: the testimony of the Lord is sure, making wise the simple: the statutes of the Lord are right, rejoicing the heart: the commandment of the Lord is pure, enlightening the eyes." For, though he also comprehends other uses of the law, yet he suggests, in general, that, since God's invitation of all nations to him by the view of heaven and earth is ineffectual, this is the peculiar school of the children of God. The same is adverted to in the twenty-ninth Psalm, where the Psalmist, having preached the terrors of the Divine voice, which in thunders, in winds, in showers, in whirlwinds, and in tempests, shakes the earth, makes the mountains tremble, and breaks the cedars, adds, at length, towards the close, "in his temple doth every one speak of his glory;" because unbelievers are deaf to all the voices of God, which resound in the air. So, in another Psalm, after describing the terrible waves of the sea, he concludes thus: "Thy testimonies are very sure: holiness becometh thine house, O Lord, for ever." Hence also proceeds the observation of Christ to the Samaritan woman, that her nation and all others worshipped they knew not what; and that the Jews were the only worshippers of the true God. For, since the human mind is unable, through its imbecility, to attain any knowledge of God without the assistance of his sacred word, all mankind, except the Jews, as they sought God without the word, must necessarily have been wandering in vanity and error.

8.

The Testimony of the Spirit Necessary to Confirm the Scripture, In Order to the Complete Establishment of Its Authority. The Suspension of Its Authority on the Judgment of the Church, an Impious Fiction.

Before I proceed any further, it is proper to introduce some remarks on the authority of the Scripture, not only to prepare the mind to regard it with due reverence, but also to remove every doubt. For, when it is admitted to be a declaration of the word of God, no man can be so deplorably presumptuous, unless he be also destitute of common sense and of the common feelings of men, as to dare to derogate from the credit due to the speaker. But since we are not favoured with daily oracles from heaven, and since it is only in the Scriptures that the Lord hath been pleased to preserve his truth in perpetual remembrance, it obtains the same complete credit and authority with believers, when they are satisfied of its divine origin, as if they heard the very words pronounced by God himself. The subject, indeed, merits a diffuse discussion, and a most accurate examination. But the reader will pardon me, if I attend rather to what the design of this work admits, than to what the extensive nature of the present subject requires. But there has very generally prevailed a most pernicious error, that the Scriptures have only so much weight as is conceded to them by the suffrages of the Church; as though the eternal and inviolable truth of God depended on the arbitrary will of men. For thus, with great contempt of the Holy Spirit, they inquire, Who can assure us that God is the author of them? Who can with certainty affirm, that they have been preserved safe and uncorrupted to the present age? Who can persuade us that this book ought to be received with reverence, and that expunged from the sacred number, unless all these things were regulated by the decisions of the Church? It depends, therefore, (say they,) on the determination of the Church, to decide both what reverence is due to the Scripture, and what books are to be comprised in its canon. Thus, sacrilegious men, while they wish to introduce an unlimited tyranny, under the name of the Church, are totally unconcerned with what absurdities they embarrass themselves and others, provided they can extort from the ignorant this one admission, that the Church can do everything. But, if this be true, what will be the condition of those wretched consciences, which are seeking a solid assurance of eternal life, if all the promises extant concerning it rest only on the judgment of men? Will the reception of such an answer cause their fluctuations to subside, and their terrors to vanish? Again, how will the impious ridicule our faith, and all men call it in question, if it be understood to possess only a precarious authority depending on the favour of men!

II. But such cavilers are completely refuted even by one word of the Apostle. He testifies that the church is "built upon the foundation of the apostles and prophets." If the doctrine of the prophets and apostles be the foundation of the Church, it must have been certain, antecedently to the existence of the Church. Nor is there any foundation for this cavil, that though the Church derive its origin from the Scriptures, yet it remains doubtful what writings are to be ascribed to the prophets and apostles, unless it be determined by the Church. For if the Christian Church has been from the beginning founded on the writings of the prophets and the preaching of the apostles, wherever that doctrine is found, the approbation of it has certainly preceded the formation of the Church; since without it the Church itself had never existed. It is a very false notion, therefore, that the power of judging of the Scripture belongs to the Church, so as to make the certainty of it dependent on the Church's will. Wherefore, when the Church receives it, and seals it with her suffrage, she does not authenticate a thing otherwise dubious or controvertible; but, knowing it to be the truth of her God, performs a duty of piety, by treating it with immediate veneration. But, with regard to the question, How shall we be persuaded of its divine original, unless we have recourse to the decree of the Church? this is just as if any one should inquire, How shall we learn to distinguish light from darkness, white from black, sweet from bitter? For the Scripture exhibits as clear evidence of its truth, as white and black things do of their colour, or sweet and bitter things of their taste.

III. I know, indeed, that they commonly cite the opinion of Augustine, where he says, "that he would not believe the Gospel unless he were influenced by the authority of the Church." But how falsely and unfairly this is cited in support of such a notion, it is easy to discover from the context. He was in that contending with the Manichees, who wished to be credited, without any controversy, when they affirmed the truth to be on their side, but never proved it. Now, as they made the authority of the Gospel a pretext in order to establish the credit of their Manichæus, he inquires what they would do if they met with a man who did not believe the Gospel; with what kind of persuasion, they would convert him to their opinion. He afterwards adds, "Indeed, I would not give credit to the Gospel," &c., intending, that he himself, when an alien from the faith, could not be prevailed on to embrace the Gospel as the certain truth of God, till he was convinced by the authority of the Church. And is it surprising that any one, yet destitute of the knowledge of Christ, should pay a respect to men? Augustine, therefore, does not there maintain that the faith of the pious is founded on the authority of the Church, nor does he mean that the certainty of the Gospel depends on it; but simply, that unbelievers would have no assurance of the truth of the Gospel, that would win them to Christ, unless they were influenced by the consent of the Church. And a little before, he clearly confirms it in these words: "When I shall have commended my own creed, and derided yours, what judgment, think you, ought we to form, what conduct ought we to pursue, but to forsake those who invite us to acknowledge things that are certain, and afterwards command us to believe things that are uncertain; and to follow those who invite us first to believe what we cannot yet clearly see, that, being strengthened by faith, we may acquire an understanding of what we believe; our mind being now internally strengthened and illuminated, not by men, but by God himself?" These are the express words of Augustine; whence the inference is obvious to everyone, that this holy man did not design to suspend our faith in the Scriptures on the arbitrary decision of the Church, but only to show (what we all confess to be true) that they who are yet unilluminated by the Spirit of God, are, by a reverence for the Church, brought to such a docility as to submit to learn the faith of Christ from the Gospel; and that thus the authority of the Church is an introduction to prepare us for the faith of the Gospel. For we see that he will have the certainty of the pious to rest on a very different foundation. Otherwise, I do not deny his frequently urging on the Manichees the universal consent of the Church, with a view to prove the truth of the

Scripture, which they rejected. Whence his rebuke of Faustus, "for not submitting to the truth of the Gospel, so founded, so established, so gloriously celebrated, and delivered through certain successions from the apostolic age." But he nowhere insinuates that the authority which we attribute to the Scripture depends on the definitions or decrees of men: he only produces the universal judgment of the Church, which was very useful to his argument, and gave him an advantage over his adversaries. If anyone desire a fuller proof of this, let him read his treatise "Of the Advantage of Believing;" where he will find, that he recommends no other facility of believing, than such as may afford us an introduction, and be a proper beginning of inquiry, as he expresses himself; yet that we should not be satisfied with mere opinion, but rest upon certain and solid truth.

IV. It must be maintained, as I have before asserted, that we are not established in the belief of the doctrine till we are indubitably persuaded that God is its Author. The principal proof, therefore, of the Scriptures is every where derived from the character of the Divine Speaker. The prophets and apostles boast not of their own genius, or any of those talents which conciliate the faith of the hearers; nor do they insist on arguments from reason; but bring forward the sacred name of God, to compel the submission of the whole world. We must now see how it appears, not from probable supposition, but from clear demonstration, that this use of the divine name is neither rash nor fallacious. Now, if we wish to consult the true interest of our consciences; that they may not be unstable and wavering, the subjects of perpetual doubt; that they may not hesitate at the smallest scruples,—this persuasion must be sought from a higher source than human reasons, or judgments, or conjectures—even from the secret testimony of the Spirit. It is true that, if we were inclined to argue the point, many things might be adduced which certainly evince, if there be any God in heaven, that he is the Author of the Law, and the Prophecies, and the Gospel. Even though men of learning and deep judgment rise up in opposition, and exert and display all the powers of their minds in this dispute, yet, unless they are wholly lost to all sense of shame, this confession will be extorted from them, that the Scripture exhibits the plainest evidences that it is God who speaks in it, which manifests its doctrine to be divine. And we shall soon see, that all the books of the sacred Scripture very far excel all other writings. If we read it with pure eyes and sound minds, we shall immediately perceive the majesty of God, which will subdue our audacious contradictions, and compel us to obey him. Yet it is acting a preposterous part, to endeavour to produce sound faith in the Scripture by disputations. Though, indeed, I am far from excelling in peculiar dexterity or eloquence, yet, if I were to contend with the most subtle despisers of God, who are ambitious to display their wit and their skill in weakening the authority of Scripture, I trust I should be able, without difficulty, to silence their obstreperous clamour. And, if it were of any use to attempt a refutation of their cavils, I would easily demolish the boasts which they mutter in secret corners. But though any one vindicates the sacred word of God from the aspersions of men, yet this will not fix in their hearts that assurance which is essential to true piety. Religion appearing, to profane men, to consist wholly in opinion, in order that they may not believe anything on foolish or slight grounds, they wish and expect it to be proved by rational arguments, that Moses and the prophets spake by divine inspiration. But I reply, that the testimony of the Spirit is superior to all reason. For, as God alone is a sufficient witness of himself in his own word, so also the word will never gain credit in the hearts of men, till it be confirmed by the internal testimony of the Spirit. It is necessary, therefore, that the same Spirit, who spake by the mouths of the prophets, should penetrate into our hearts, to convince us that they faithfully delivered the oracles which were divinely intrusted to them. And this connection is very suitably expressed in these words: "My Spirit that is upon thee, and my word which I have put in thy mouth, shall not depart out of thy mouth, nor out of the mouth of thy seed, nor out of the mouth of thy seed's seed, for ever." Some good men are troubled that they are not always prepared with clear proof to oppose the impious, when they murmur with impunity against the divine word; as though the Spirit were not therefore denominated a "seal," and "an earnest," for the confirmation of the faith of the pious; because, till he illuminate their minds, they are perpetually fluctuating amidst a multitude of doubts.

V. Let it be considered, then, as an undeniable truth, that they who have been inwardly taught by the Spirit, feel an entire acquiescence in the Scripture, and that it is self-authenticated, carrying with it its own evidence, and ought not to be made the subject of demonstration and arguments from reason; but it obtains the credit which it deserves with us by the testimony of the Spirit. For though it conciliates our reverence by its internal majesty, it never seriously affects us till it is confirmed by the Spirit in our hearts. Therefore, being illuminated by him, we now believe the divine original of the Scripture, not from our own judgment or that of others, but we esteem the certainty, that we have received it from God's own mouth by the ministry of men, to be superior to that of any human judgment, and equal to that of an intuitive perception of God himself in it. We seek not arguments or probabilities to support our judgment, but submit our judgments and understandings as to a thing concerning which it is impossible for us to judge; and that not like some persons, who are in the habit of hastily embracing what they do not understand, which displeases them as soon as they examine it, but because we feel the firmest conviction that we hold an invincible truth; nor like those unhappy men who surrender their minds captives to superstitions, but because we perceive in it the undoubted energies of the Divine power, by which we are attracted and inflamed to an understanding and voluntary obedience, but with a vigour and efficacy superior to the power of any human will or knowledge. With the greatest justice, therefore, God exclaims by Isaiah, that the prophets and all the people were his witnesses; because, being taught by prophecies, they were certain that God had spoken without the least fallacy or ambiguity. It is such a persuasion, therefore, as requires no reasons; such a knowledge as is supported by the highest reason, in which, indeed, the mind rests with greater security and constancy than in any reasons; it is, finally, such a sentiment as cannot be produced but by a revelation from heaven. I speak of nothing but what every believer experiences in his heart, except that my language falls far short of a just explication of the subject. I pass over many things at present, because this subject will present itself for discussion again in another place. Only let it be known here, that that alone is true faith which the Spirit of God seals in our hearts. And with this one reason every reader of modesty and docility will be satisfied: Isaiah predicts that "all the children" of the renovated Church "shall be taught of God." Herein God deigns to confer a singular privilege on his elect, whom he distinguishes from the rest of mankind. For what is the beginning of true learning but a prompt alacrity to hear the voice of God? By the mouth of Moses he demands our attention in these terms: "Say not in thine heart, Who shall ascend into heaven? or, Who shall descend into the deep? The word is even in thy mouth." If God hath determined that this treasury of wisdom shall be reserved for his children, it is neither surprising nor absurd, that we see so much ignorance and stupidity among the vulgar herd of mankind. By this appellation I designate even those of the greatest talents and highest rank, till they are incorporated into the Church. Moreover, Isaiah, observing that the prophetical doctrine would be incredible, not only to aliens, but also to the Jews, who wished to be esteemed members of the family, adds, at the same time, the reason—Because the arm of the Lord will not be revealed to all. Whenever, therefore, we are disturbed at the paucity of believers, let us, on the other hand, remember that none, but those to whom it was given, have any apprehension of the mysteries of God.

Note

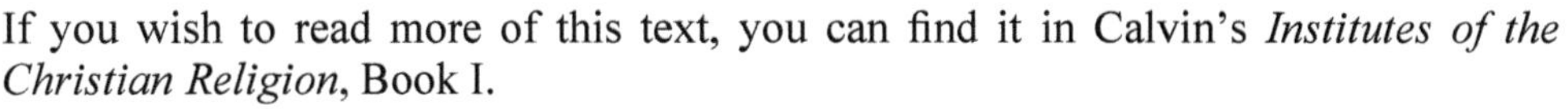

If you wish to read more of this text, you can find it in Calvin's *Institutes of the Christian Religion*, Book I.

Enjoyed your Christian reading?

Don't end your introduction to Christian literature here.

Send a blank email to

thegoodchristian10@gmail.com

for access to Christian audiobooks.